ILLUSTRATING ARCHITECTURE

ALBERT LORENZ

VNR VAN NOSTRAND REINHOLD COMPANY
_____ *New York*

For
Maureen
Margaret
Kirsten

Printed in the United States of America

Published by Van Nostrand Reinhold Company Inc.
135 West 50th Street
New York, New York 10020

Van Nostrand Reinhold Company Limited
Molly Millars Lane
Wokingham, Berkshire RG11 2PY, England

Van Nostrand Reinhold
480 La Trobe Street
Melbourne, Victoria 3000, Australia

Macmillan of Canada
Division of Gage Publishing Limited
164 Commander Boulevard
Agincourt, Ontario M1S 3C7, Canada

16 15 14 13 12 11 10 9 8 7 6 5 4 3 2 1

Library of Congress Cataloging in Publication Data

Lorenz, Albert, 1941–
    Illustrating architecture.

    1. Architectural drawing. 2. Architectural rendering.
I. Title.
NA2700.L56 1985   720'.28'4   84–19498
ISBN 0–442–25973–5

Contents

1. Setting Up   7

2. Linework and Value   15

3. Shade and Shadow   27

4. Trees   35

5. People   45

6. Elevations—Plans—Sections   51

7. Methods of Perspective   65

8. Plan Perspective—Section Perspective   71

9. Photographic Perspective   79

10. Erasing, Cutting in, Making Changes   87

11. Aerial Technique   91

12. Multi-photo Technique   99

13. Color   105

14. Textures   111

15. Charts   117

16. Photo-Drawing Montage   125

17. Cartoons   137

18. Overviews   149

Acknowledgments

The Studio 1971–1984

Valmi Bartoli
Jimmie Bly
Dennis Camps
Anthony Caradonna
Vincent Cortina
Ross Cromarty
Michael Davis
Robert DeRonde
Ann Dougherty
Rob Esquivel
Alfredo Estabenéz
Humberto J. Fontana
Nancy Gallagher
Michael Greer
Christopher Guerra
Osamu Hashimoto
Anna Hertzberg
Tom Holian
Igal
Kevin Johnson
Jaan Kangro
Stephen Kiely
Peter Kukresh
Peter Kurth
Sinnikka Laine
Anita Lee
Peter Leth
Leonard C. Lizak
José Martinéz
Anne-Marie McCartney
Jean McCartney
Thomas Mohr
Steven Morgan

Patrick P. Murphy
Patricia Musguire-Danker
John Nastasi
Natalie Newey
Andrew Neuberger
Olesh
Andrew Piatek
Peter Primak
Harry Prushansky
Nina Reese
Gary Rogers
Scott Ross
Peter Sahmel
Rick Scott
Gary Slutsky
Kathy Spalding
Victoria Steven
Peter Szule
Adrian Tolsch
Hooker Van Deusen
Frank Vertin
Nancy Vigneau
Steve Wadsworth
Lynn Weaver
Winston Whittaker
Gary Wilson
Robert Wolf
Christian Mathieu Xatrec
William Young
Robert Zaccone
Carlos E. Zapata
Gil Zarins

Introduction

Over the years, I have read numerous books on drawing, both as a student and later as a professional. Many were interesting and enlightening; some were quite dull. The interesting books shared certain characteristics: they had a varied approach to illustration, and they presented an array of drawings, thereby increasing the reader's understanding of illustration by allowing him/her to view professional artwork. On the following pages, I will present as many examples as possible of both my work and that of my students. I will explain each illustration's personality, including the media, dimensions, execution time and methods applied. Hopefully, the reader will then be able to learn by seeing, and finally by doing, drawings.

It must be understood that all of the drawings presented in this book were produced by a studio. As one would expect, the only difference between a studio and the lone illustrator is that a studio has several artists working together to produce an illustration, rather than just one artist. For many reasons I prefer to have a studio. First, I enjoy working with people more than I do working alone. Second, more work can be accomplished in a shorter amount of time. Therefore, I am not forced to turn down jobs that I would really like to do because I am presently working on another job. Third, because of my teaching schedule, I cannot be at the studio all of the time; when I am teaching, other artists are there to carry on the work. Last, but most important, I like the give and take of criticism and the infusion of new ideas that is inherent to the life of a studio.

I began my studio after I reached the conclusion that working from 9 to 5 in an architectural office was definitely not for me. I have always loved drawing and architecture but was never suited to the routine of an architectural office. The wonderful thing about my studio is that it has always included people who love architecture *and* drawing.

When I first established my studio the work was confined strictly to architectural illustration. That changed very gradually, and the studio expanded its limits to include advertising, magazine, editorial, newspaper, and children's book illustrations.

A studio that produces illustrations must, of course, retain a character, a recognized style of drawing. This particular character or style, which is expressed in every illustration produced, can develop only with time, experience, and hard work. It results directly from doing many drawings. An illustrator must envision what the final drawing will look like before he/she begins working. This ability comes only with experience, and that is why I believe any book on drawing must have as many images as possible.

Because I head the studio and oversee every drawing produced, it is natural that the studio's character or style be primarily the one I had chosen: pen and ink. However, I have always incorporated the best talents of the artists working with me to expand and enrich the character or style of the studio. Being able to pool creative talents is one of the studio's greatest advantages.

Pen and ink have been the primary media used, although other media have been used successfully. My studio approaches each job differently, depending on the nature of the job and the time constraints involved. The resulting illustration retains a recognizable character that is peculiar to *this* studio, and every person who works with me is taught this method: a process of overlaying lines and stippling (dots) is used to produce textures, shades, and shadows. Once a black-and-white drawing is completed, transparent colors are added over the ink lines. Because the ink is waterproof, the lines do not blur.

1. SETTING UP

It is very exciting to commit yourself to a career as an illustrator and to live by your drawing ability. Once this decision has been made, the more mundane aspects of freelance illustration take over: how to go about getting work; how to get paid; where to buy materials; and what kind to buy.

In order to have a career as an illustrator, you must first get work. In order to get work, you must have a portfolio. Your portfolio is a brief presentation of your most outstanding, and therefore most representative, work. It is not a presentation of every drawing you have ever done. Remember to be brief and dramatic. A portfolio is usually a loose-leaf plastic page assembly. They come in all sizes, but 8 by 10 inches or 11 by 14 inches are the most commonly used sizes, as these are the standard photographic sizes.

It is not wise to present original work, so you must have your work photographed or photostatted. Insert it into a portfolio page, and you are ready to go out and get your first job. Before you do so, however, there are several questions you must ask yourself: Who are you going to see? Will this office want to see you? Do they need freelance illustrators? There is a simple way to find out the answers to these questions: an an-nouncement of your intentions in the form of a mailing piece. This announcement must interest your prospective client. It must show an example of your work and make the client want to work with you.

You should follow up this mailing with as many personal visits as possible. Do not lose faith! In the beginning, it will be difficult; jobs will not come quickly, but they will eventually come. When they do, you must be ready for them. Not only should you be prepared to complete an illustration; you must be prepared to get paid for it. *Always* have a written agreement with your client. This contract should state the due date, the price, and a brief description of the drawing itself. Always try to get a small percentage as a down payment, to defray the cost of materials, postage, and the like. Once the contract has been signed and you have a down payment, you are ready to begin the job.

Materials are the next problem. What and where should you buy? No matter where in the world you are, art supplies are expensive. You must establish a shopping list and find the cheapest available sources of supplies. I have tried to establish a minimal shopping list but I really cannot give you a complete list of suppliers. You will have to assemble this yourself.

Materials

The following materials are those that I use daily. They are not the only materials with which to draw, but they are the ones which I have come to depend upon.

Pens-Pencils-Inks-Dyes-Watercolors

Pens: My feeling is that all technical pen point sections will eventually break down from use, or lack of use and will have to be replaced. However, I find the only points I consistently have trouble with are points three-zero and finer (four-zero, five-zero). The finer the point, the more zeroes. I really do not advise using anything finer than five-zero. I have found Rapidograph to be the most reliable technical pen.

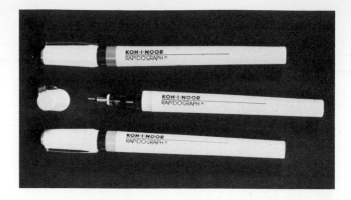

Pencils: My personal preference is to use a wood pencil (Rexel Cumberland). Layouts are usually done with nothing harder than a 2H and nothing softer than an HB. If you like using mechanical pencils, go right ahead. Personally, I love the smell of cedar.

Ink: Pelikan, in my opinion, makes the best black ink. The problem with the technical pens, of course, is clogging, so the manufacturers usually advise special black inks to be used in their pens. These inks usually have additives to allow them to flow more freely. The trouble is they are not as black or as waterproof as

Pelikan (yellow label). Pelikan does, however, clog more easily. When you use Pelikan, you must therefore clean your pens more frequently. The fact that Pelikan is waterproof is extremely important, since you will be applying watercolor washes right over the ink.

Colored Inks: I believe that Pelikan produces the finest-quality colored inks. The colors do not fade, and they are easy to apply with pen, brush, or airbrush. They mix well with other water-base colors. As with most water-base colors, they darken markedly when you use fixative over them. Remember when applying any color, especially with a spray (airbrush), to always test the resultant color with fixative before you use it.

Dyes: Brand names Luma and Dr. Martin's are both of equal quality, I feel. I both like and dislike dyes. I like them for their variety and brilliance of color. I

dislike them because they are rather difficult to apply over large areas with a brush and because they tend to fade rather quickly. They are best used in an airbrush. After using, make sure of two things. First, they must be fixed. Second, do not put the original illustration in direct sunlight, or it will fade, right in front of your eyes.

Natural Pigment Watercolors: Smooth washes; no brush strokes; a sky; a smooth background—these effects all call for natural pigment watercolors. The colors are not as brilliant as inks or dyes. The best quality is Windsor Newton, but Pelikan and Maribu are acceptable substitutes.

Watercolor Pencils: Caran D'ache makes the best watercolor pencils. These are extremely useful because they allow you to apply washes to very small areas. The method of application is simple: first apply the color with the pencil, then work the water over the pencil strokes with a brush. A good feature of these pencils is that they allow you to dull the color slightly by simply erasing, with a plastic eraser.

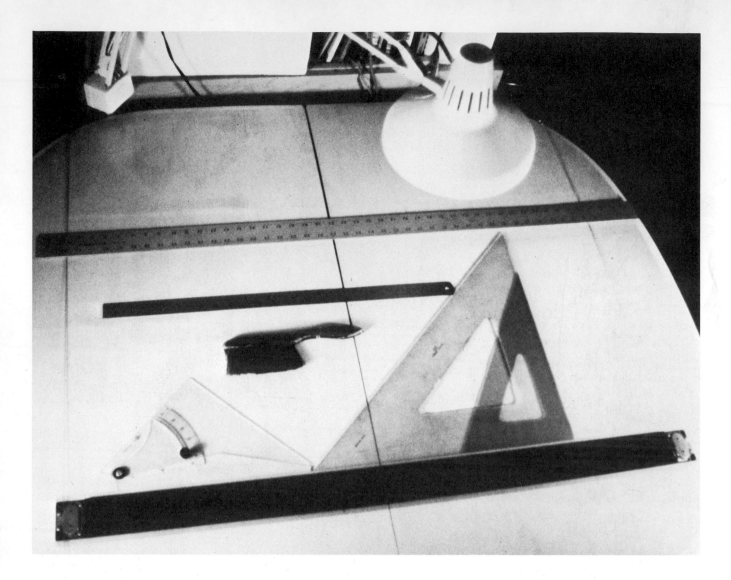

Straight Edges - Triangles - Rulers

Parallels: I believe a 42-inch parallel is the perfect size for most illustrators. I find Mayline to be the best brand.

Triangles: No bevel edges, no inking edges—you need a regular right-angle edge triangle, a 45°, a 30°, a 60°, and an adjustable triangle. You should get one large (12-inch to 24-inch) and one small (12-inch and under). You will also need a 12-inch adjustable triangle. Get clear plastic, do not get colors; they will only give you a headache.

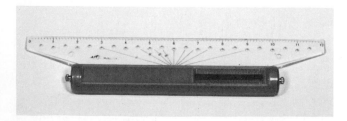

Ruler: A 24-inch steel ruler is best. I like Morilla's steel ruler because of its thickness (1/16-inch). When cutting with a matte knife, it is safer to use this steel ruler. The thickness makes it less likely that your blade will ride up and over the ruler onto your fingers, which not only hurts, but will interrupt your work.

Roller Ruler: I recommend a small (12-inch) plastic parallel. This small portable parallel allows you to draw parallel lines in any direction. It is made by Alvin.

Paper and Board

Tracing Paper: Many types of tracing paper are available, with prices ranging from inexpensive to very, very expensive. The difference in price, of course, depends upon the quality of the paper and the use to which it will be put.

Thumb Nail Paper: This is very cheap tracing paper that is sold in rolls. I use this for rough overlays, for covering drawings, for wiping up, and for any nonpermanent work. I really do not like this paper for overlays that require precision, since it is difficult to see through, tears very easily, and makes erasing impossible.

Parchment Tracing Paper: This is an inexpensive overlay paper that comes in pads. I use this paper often, since it is easy to see through. I like the idea of a pad rather than a roll because it is easier to store and more economical. I do not advise using pen and ink on this type of paper because it tears so easily. It is a very brittle paper and does not erase well.

Albanene: This 100 percent rag tracing paper is very expensive, its cost dependent upon its width and length. It may be purchased in rolls, pads, or individual sheets. This is a high-quality paper used for finished drawings in ink or pencil. It is long-lasting and erasable. Always remember that this paper must be prepared for ink. You must use an inking ground, a procedure that will be described later.

Crescent Illustration Board: I use this board because it is 100 percent rag, meaning that it is 100 percent drawing paper throughout. Many types of illustration board that are not 100 percent rag will have one or two layers of good drawing paper backed with cardboard. If you are forced to erase an ink line, you will have to remove the surface of the board and the gray cardboard underneath will show. With a 100 percent rag board, an erasure shows white drawing paper throughout. In addition, this board is sold either single thickness or double thickness. I prefer the double thickness because it will not warp when water is used or when weather conditions change. The other characteristic to look for when purchasing drawing paper or board is the tooth or relative roughness of the surface. This can vary from a highly textured watercolor paper to a glossy, magazine-finish smoothness. I always work with a medium roughness, since I find it takes not only pen and ink, but wet media the best.

Bristol Board: This board is not only 100 percent rag, but flexible, too. One advantage of this board is that it comes in varying thicknesses called plys; one-ply, two-ply, three-ply, and up. If you hold two-ply bristol up to the light, you can see through it. This means that you can do a layout on tracing paper, as an underlay, and be able to do that drawing on two-ply by tracing over the paper. You must, of course, work with a light source under the tracing paper, which means you must have a light table. This paper or board also comes in varying degrees of roughness or tooth. Generally, I would advise a board that is in between— neither too rough nor too smooth.

Erasers

Since we all make mistakes, erasers are a must. For ordinary pencil I use a Staedtler Mars plastic eraser, since it leaves no color and does not hurt the surface of the board. For ink lines I use a K & E electric eraser, which I find to be the best. Removing ink from board is relatively simple as long as you are working on a 100 percent rag board. The difficulty with erasing anything always comes after the fact. If you have to apply a wash to the illustration, you must do it very carefully or the area where you have erased, which now has a different texture, will show.

Special Tools

Skum-X: This rather oddly named powder is made by Dietzgen. It is sprinkled on a drawing to keep it from getting dirty—not to clean it. Your triangles and drafting tools will roll over the paper on top of the Skum-X granules. Skum-X may be purchased either in a bag or a container. Use the container, rather than the bag, since the granules are too fine in the bag and will stop your pens.

Pounce: Pounce is a powder used on tracing paper that is 100 percent rag and has an oil finish; it is difficult to ink on a surface like this, so it must be prepared. Sprinkle pounce on the paper, rub it in, and then the ink can be applied more easily. Do not confuse this with Skum-X, as it will not keep your drawing clean.

Glue: There are times when you must glue one piece of paper or board to another, as for a mistake or an addition. Always use rubber cement. It should be the texture of tomato juice. Apply it to both the surfaces that are to be glued. You can thin rubber cement by using rubber cement thinner (benzine). Always use a glass jar to store your rubber cement, so that it will remain airtight. For picking up excess cement, use a piece of hard rubber, called a rubber cement pickup. For tracing paper or anything thinner than two-ply Bristol, rubber cement cannot be used because it will yellow and the color will show through the paper. The 3M Company makes a mounting adhesive sheet that is ideal, since it is not only strong but will not yellow.

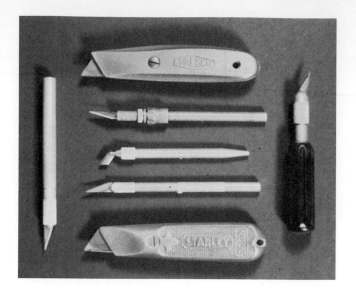

Knives: I use two types of knives. First, a matte knife for heavy cuts—cutting illustration board, mats, etc. Second, an X-acto knife for fine cuts—paper or thin board.

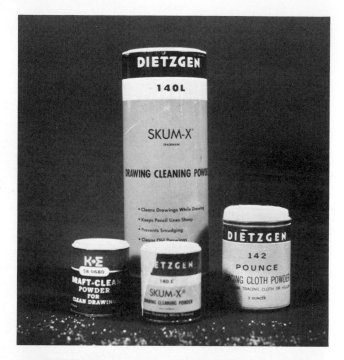

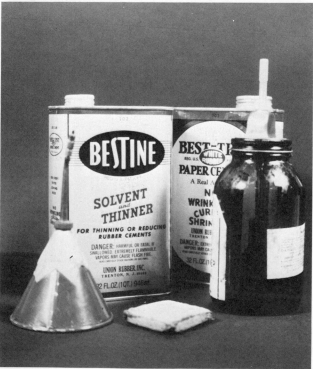

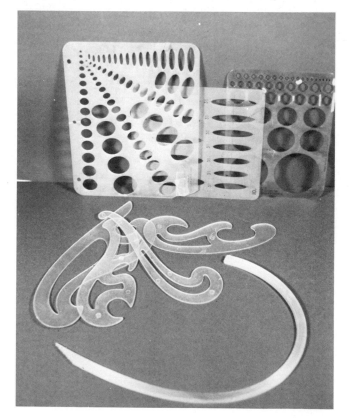

French Curves and *Adjustable Curves:* These tools give you the ability to draw just about any curve. The problem is that you will probably have to draw an infinite number of curves, so you must put together a considerable collection of French curves. I would advise you to do this bit by bit; buy the curves as you need them. The adjustable curve is made of plastic (do not buy the rubber curves, they do not hold their shape) and can be bent to any large curve you want.

Templates: Buy circles, ellipses, and other templates as you need them. They are expensive.

Light: Use something that approximates daylight as closely as possible. I use a Luxo combination neon and incandescent—expensive, but well worth the price.

Tape: Masking tape is used to hold your drawing to the drawing surface. Do not use any other kind, such as Scotch tape. Ideal thickness is ½-inch.

Towels: Always keep an old towel around to lean on, to wipe your hands on, and to clear your pens on.

Transfer Sheet: In order to get a drawing from tracing paper to illustration board, you must make a transfer sheet. It is simply a piece of tracing paper that you treat with graphite and rubber cement thinner, so that it will act like a piece of carbon paper used in typing. Simply rub a 6B graphite stick on a piece of tracing paper, sprinkle some rubber cement thinner on this, and rub it in with a tissue. This keeps the graphite on the paper and makes it less messy. Now tape your piece of transfer paper onto the illustration board, then tape the drawing to be transferred onto this. Trace over this drawing using a colored pencil (so you know what has been traced), making sure your line is coming through on the illustration board. When you have gone over all of the lines, remove the tracing paper and the transfer sheet. Your drawing will be lightly drawn in pencil on the illustration board.

Books:

I recommend the following books; I believe they give a very comprehensive understanding of the art of drawing:

Burden, Ernest. *Architectural Delineation.* New York: McGraw-Hill Book Company, 1971.

Ching, Frank. *Architectural Graphics.* New York: Van Nostrand Reinhold Company, 1975.

Coulin, Claudius. *Step-by-step Perspective Drawing, 2nd ed.* New York: Van Nostrand Reinhold Company, 1984.

D'Amelio, Joseph. *Perspective Drawing Handbook.* New York: Van Nostrand Reinhold Company, 1984.

Forseth, Kevin. *Graphics for Architecture.* New York: Van Nostrand Reinhold Company, 1980.

Gill, Robert. *VNR Manual of Rendering with Pen and Ink.* New York: Van Nostrand Reinhold Company, 1984.

Gray, Bill. *Studio Tips for Artists and Graphic Designers.* New York: Van Nostrand Reinhold Company, 1976.

Gray, Bill. *More Studio Tips.* New York: Van Nostrand Reinhold Company, 1979.

Hogarth, Paul. *Drawing Architecture: A Creative Approach.* New York: Watson Guptill Publications, 1979.

Jacoby, Helmut. *New Techniques of Architectural Rendering, 2nd ed.* New York: Van Nostrand Reinhold Company, 1981.

Lockard, William Kirby. *Design Drawing Experiences.* Tucson: Pepper Publishing, 1973.

Martin, C. Leslie. *Architectural Graphics.* New York: Macmillan Company, 1970.

Maurello, S. Ralph. *The Complete Airbrush Book.* New York: Leon Amiel Publishers, 1980.

Oles, Paul Stevenson. *Architectural Illustration.* New York: Van Nostrand Reinhold Company, 1979.

Worth, Leslie. *The Practice of Watercolour Painting.* New York: Watson-Guptill Publications, 1977.

2. LINEWORK AND VALUE

Whenever you begin an illustration, always imagine it completed. Keep this image in mind and work to make it appear in front of you. The image becomes reality through the use of lines and values. A line can be thin or thick, gray or black. Once you have drawn lines and enclosed an area, the lightness or darkness within those lines convey an idea: sunlight, shade, or shadow, for example. How do you, as an illustrator, convey these ideas? How is brick drawn to show that it is in sunshine or in shade or in shadow? How is glass or earth delineated under these conditions?

There is, of course, no one way to illustrate, no one way to achieve light and dark values. I will attempt to show as many examples as possible. The more you

see, the more you will understand my method of achieving line and value.

Lines can be drawn freehand or with a straightedge. There is a real difference in feeling between a freehand drawing and a straight-line drawing. The freehand drawing presents a more relaxed, loose approach to a subject. The straight-line drawing is more technical and tight in feeling.

Values are decided before the drawing is begun. They are for the most part arbitrary. Sunlight is the lightest, followed by shade, and finally shadow. The technique changes from drawing to drawing; the description of each drawing explains the technique used.

Pen and Ink
Double-thick Crescent Illustration
Board #10; 30 × 40 inches
Client: Fearon/O'Leary

This was a difficult drawing, both in its execution and its ambition. The clients needed a drawing that would present their building in a nonconventional way. They wanted to stay away from "the mundane architectural rendering." We decided to treat the elevation as a reflective and constantly changing wall of glass. We began by drawing the elevation at ³⁄₁₆ scale (approximately 40 inches tall). After the elevation was drawn in pencil (H or HB), an overlay was done in pencil to pick up highlights. Once we had what we wanted in pencil, it was time to begin to draw in ink. For pure precision and also because the drawing was to be reproduced in newspapers, halftones (any kind of wash or watercolor) had to be omitted. Stippling (round dots of ink) was chosen as the technique of completion. This is a time-consuming but exact method. The imitation of light and dark is relatively easy to achieve and precise. This illustration took approximately 100 hours to complete. It was drawn, using two-, three-, and four-zero Rapidograph pens.

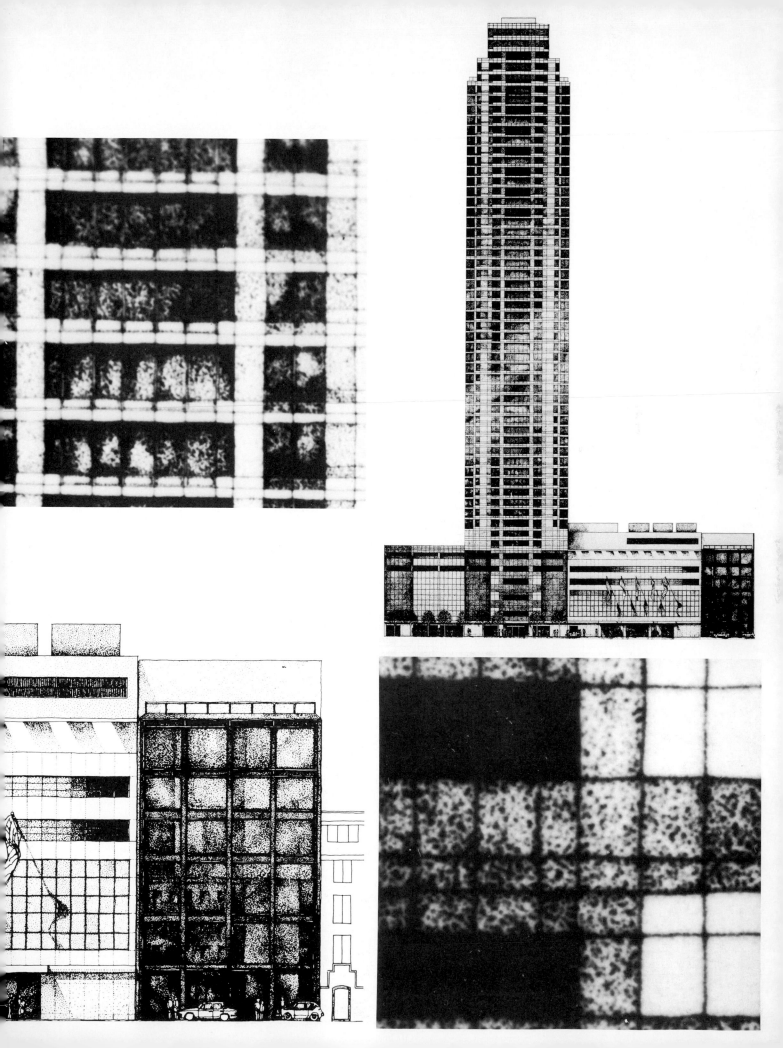

Pen and Ink
Double-thick Crescent Illustration Board #110;   20 × 30 inches
Client: Albert Lorenz

The layout was done from a slide that was projected and traced on the illustration board using a 2H pencil. The slide was put into the projector which was turned on, projecting the image onto the tracing paper or illustration board. Then, working in pencil, we simply drew everything we saw. When we turned off the projector, the image was seen on the illustration board or tracing paper. Once all details and all shading had been transferred to the illustration board, the drawing was ready to ink. Using three-zero and four-zero Rapidographs, and a combination of linework and stippling, the textures, the light, shade, and shadow were drawn. This illustration took approximately 100 hours to complete. The viewer should note how the linework was done and how the textures work together to produce the total drawing. Notice that even in the darkest areas, the values come from careful crosshatching or linework, not from brushed-on tones. With all of these drawings, take note of the textures and how they were produced and work together.

Right
Pen and Ink
Double-thick Crescent Illustration
Board;   10 × 15 inches
Client: Richard Packert
The subtlety of light and shade on
the surface of smooth metal could
only be reproduced using stippling.
You will, I am sure, see this with
more clarity in many of the drawings
that follow. This drawing took about
twenty hours and was done with a
four-zero Rapidograph.

Near right
Pen and Ink
Two-ply Bristol Board
6-inch Circle
Client: Atheneum Publishers
Stippling allows the illustrator to
make areas darker or lighter merely
by changing the spacing of the dots
of ink. The size of the dots is regu-
lated by the size of the pen being
used. Once again, the color in the
original was applied with a brush
right over the ink. Note that when
the dots are placed on the drawing,
they are perfect (or as close to perfect
as possible) circles and are placed
with great care.

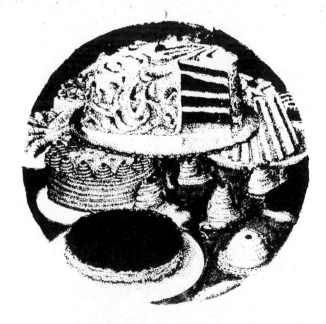

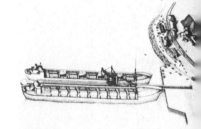

Far right
Pen and Ink
Double-thick Crescent Illustration
Board;   20 × 30 inches
Client: Jack Hough Associates
Once again, stippling was done with
a three- and four-zero Rapidograph.
This technique is ideal for land forms
and for areas where forms and light
change quickly.

Right
Pen and Ink
Two-ply Bristol Board
16 × 20 inches
Client: Kiwanis Magazine
The linework in this illustration was not done with a Rapidograph pen but with a flexible-point pen dipped into the ink. The reason for using this type of point was that we wanted a more varied line, one that changes character. The flexible point gives a less mechanical feeling. This drawing, originally in color, was done using Pelikan waterproof ink. The advantage of Pelikan ink is that once it dries, it will not spread, and a wash can be applied right over it. In this case, the color was applied with a Windsor Newton Red Sable #7 brush over the pen and ink. The color was done using a combination of Pelikan inks, Luma Dyes, and natural pigment watercolors.

URBAN DECAY

Pen and Ink
Double-thick Crescent Illustration
Board;   20 × 30 inches
Client: Albert Lorenz

This editorial on the state of the city was done in about seventy to seventy-five hours, using three-, four-, and five-zero pens. The textures were achieved by combining stippling and linework. Notice that the insects and animals in the foreground do not blend with the background at all because they were drawn with a three-zero pen, while the buildings behind them were drawn with a five-zero pen. The actual buildings in Brooklyn Heights and lower Manhattan were constructed using several photographs.

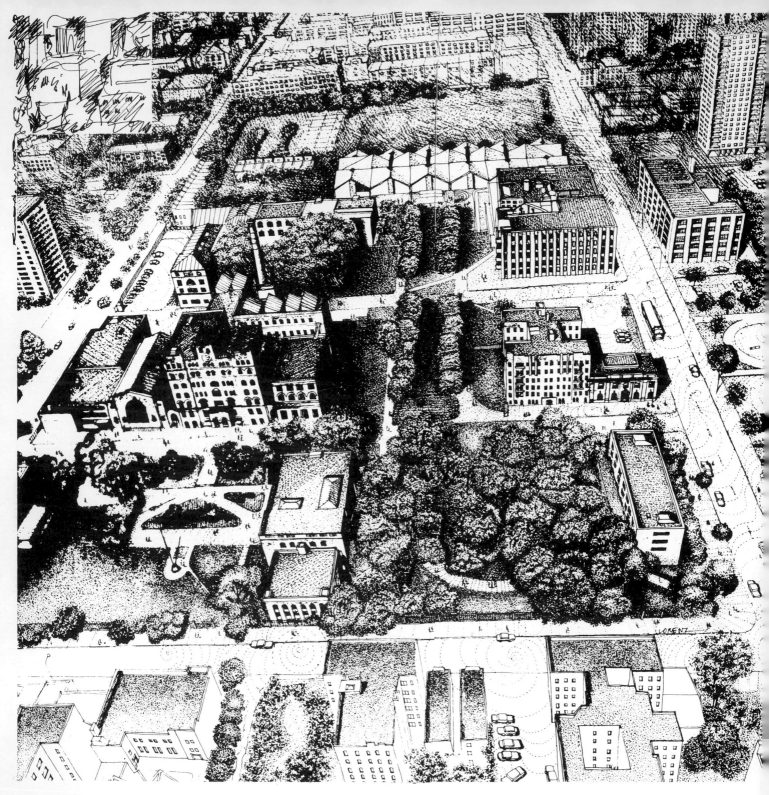

Pen and Ink
Two-ply Bristol Board
30 × 40 inches
Client: Pratt Institute

This overview of the Pratt Institute campus was done in pen and ink (three-, four-, and five-zero). The layout was done by using a photograph taken with a wide-angle lens. Since there was quite a bit of distortion at the edges of the picture, we had to make visual corrections. Whenever doing an illustration, it is important to constantly look at the illustration with a critical eye. Always make sure your work looks the way you visualized it. Do not be lazy, do not accept less than your best effort. Once the visual corrections were made, we began the final illustration. In this case, we were working on two-ply Bristol board (kid finish). Kid finish is of medium roughness. The layout was done on tracing paper and was transferred to the Bristol by means of a light table. The Bristol (up to two-ply) was thin enough to see through, making it simple to trace right through the tracing paper (underlay) and transfer the illustration to the Bristol. Once transferred, applying the ink was the next challenge. This drawing was done freehand, without instruments.

Before the freehand part of the drawing was done in ink, an underdrawing was completed in pencil, using instruments. The underdrawing was a straight-line drawing. Whenever I refer to a drawing as being done freehand, it is always done in this manner. The ink linework for this drawing was done using a four- and a five-zero pen. You will see that the textures themselves are a mixture of stippling in varying degrees of density. The density varies so that the viewer's eye will move over the drawing. If the textures are always the same, the drawing will appear flat and stagnant.

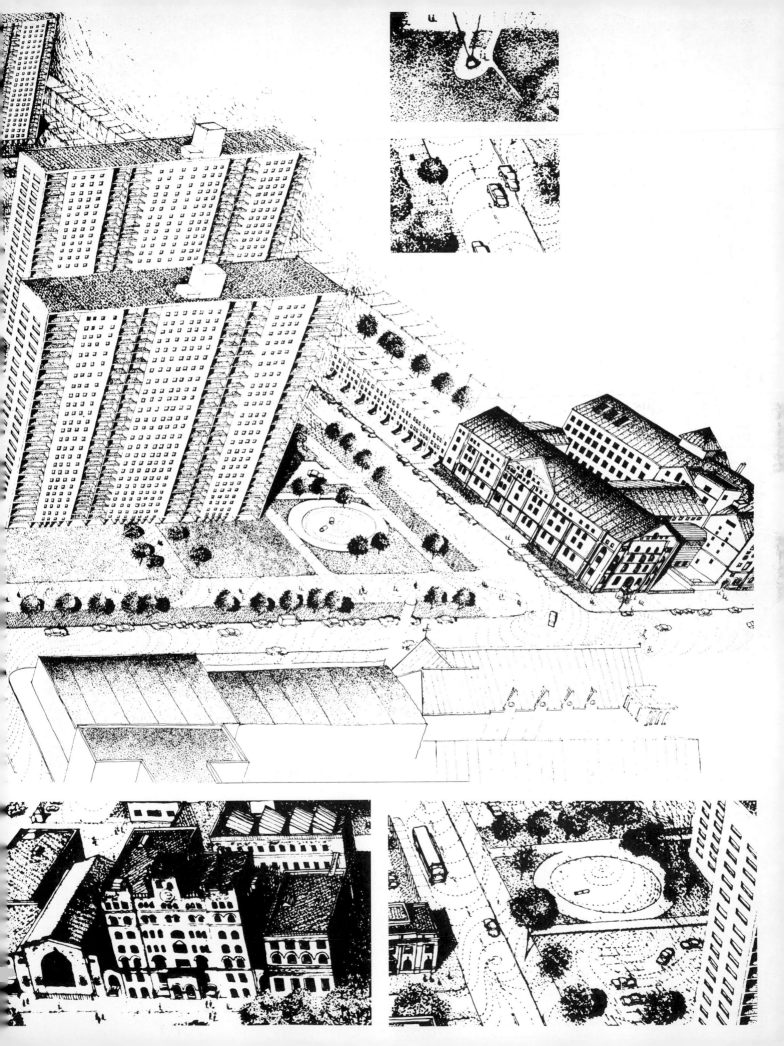

3. SHADE AND SHADOW

Illustrations depend upon the delineation of light, shade, and shadow for drama and for the appearance of reality. My method of drawing dictates that I work with pen and ink to imitate the effects of light by means of linework, stippling, and ink washes.

I have some personal rules that I follow when building textures for shade and shadow. First, set a value scale. Shadow is always the darkest value, followed by shade, and then the light value. This is an arbitrary scale, but it provides a framework from which to start. Each material must be delineated differently. For example, shadow on a brick surface must be treated differently from shadow on a steel surface. I always make

my decision as to how different materials will be drawn before I begin the final drawing. I do small sections of the final drawing on another piece of board, so I know how each area will be handled in the final drawing. By doing this, you will have an alphabet of textures. With this alphabet you will be able to produce all of the textures that will make up your drawing.

It really does not matter whether your drawing is freehand or straightedge. The values are always achieved by overlaying lines or by stippling until the correct value is achieved. Take note of how the following drawings achieve the value of various materials, in sunlight, shade, and shadow.

Top, left
Colored Pencil
Albanene Tracing Paper
15 × 20 inches
Client: Kenyon & Eckhardt
Pencil on tracing paper, bold shadows, and a feeling of light give this drawing its drama. Caran D'ache water-base pencils were used in combination with Prismacolor pencils.

Bottom
Pen and Ink
Double-thick Crescent Illustration Board; 8 × 10 inches
Client: Warren Gran Associates
Here is a sketch-type technique, in which shade and shadow are indicated by the use of a bold line and an ink wash. The wash was applied with a brush. When applying the ink, do it evenly and do not let it dry in puddles, as it will warp the surface of the board or paper. After the ink has dried, erase it lightly. This will take the shine off the ink and give a uniform finish to the drawing.

Left
Pen and Ink
Two-ply Bristol Board
24 x 36 inches
Client: Philip Johnson
This eye-level illustration was done freehand. The drama in this illustration was achieved by applying a very light gray wash behind the building. The reflection on the street not only gives the feeling of a recent rainfall, but also gives the drawing a base on which to sit.

Below
Pen and Ink
Two-ply Bristol Board
15 × 20 inches
Client: Harper & Row
This drawing consists almost entirely of stippled textures, but you should notice that different materials are delineated by the varying density of the stippling and by the size of the pen used. In other words, even though the same technique was used throughout the drawing, changing the spacing and the size of the dots changed the character of the drawing.

Pen and Ink
Double-thick Illustration Board
24 × 17 inches
Client: Albert Lorenz
This drawing took about 100 hours to complete. It was done using three-, four-, and five-zero Rapidographs. The layout was done using two slides that were projected onto an illustration board.

Student Work
All of these drawings, done by my
students, share one major positive
characteristic: they all delineate the
effects of light extremely well. They
are dramatic drawings because of the
way in which they represent architectural materials and the effect of
light, shade, and shadow on them.
Note the positive characteristics of
each illustration and file them in the
drawing area of your brain. Be ready
to pull them out when you need
them.

4. TREES

It is wise to assume that anyone who looks at a drawing is graphically sophisticated. After all, people look at all kinds of graphics and drawings every day of their lives. Textbooks, magazines, and television all bring professional illustration to the viewer. It is very important, therefore, that the illustrations that architects and designers present to either their clients or the public attain this same professional level. Any illustration is made up of many components, and all must be drawn with the same care and professionalism. For instance, I have seen many illustrations in which the building appears to sit in the middle of a deserted city, with no cars, trees, or people in sight. It is important that the supporting elements of an illustration be as well drawn, and as accurate, as the major portions of the illustration. These elements will give both character and mood to the illustration.

Let us begin with trees. Because I believe the surroundings must attain the same detail and accuracy that the buildings do, I draw each leaf or I give the viewer the feeling that each leaf was drawn. Different types of trees drawn with varying amounts of detail, present a feeling of realism and make the illustration more acceptable to the viewer.

In order to be able to draw a truly realistic tree, try the following: First, always have a photograph or drawing of the tree you are about to draw in front of you; never try to draw from memory. I have a library of tree books and examples of trees, and recommend that you start one today. Next, make a light pencil drawing of the branch layout. You are now ready to begin inking. Choose your pen and begin to draw each leaf. Take note of how this is done by looking at the trees on the following pages.

Pen and Ink
Two-ply Bristol Board
16 × 22 inches
Client: National Endowment for the Humanities

The texture of the bark, and the pattern of the branches make this illustration dramatic. The texture of the bark was produced by overlapping three- and four-zero pen lines. Great care had to be taken in putting the lines down, since there were so many of them; if carelessly done, the Bristol board can actually shred. Transparent dyes were then applied with a brush right over the linework.

Below and left
Pen and Ink
Double-thick Crescent Illustration
Board;   30 × 30 inches
Client: Wiener and Gran Architects
The trees create the setting in this
illustration. Observe the leaves, the
textures, and the realism. This
drawing was done using four- and
five-zero Rapidographs. It took approximately one hundred hours to
complete.

Opposite, top
Pen and Ink
Two-ply Bristol Board
15 x 25 inches
Client: New York City Convention Center
This freehand drawing (a view of Manhattan from New Jersey) was done from a slide using three- and four-zero Rapidographs. There are no halftones in this illustration; it was designed to be used for newspaper publicity, and halftones would not have reproduced well.

This page, bottom
Pen and Ink
Double-thick Crescent Illustration Board
24 x 36 inches
Client: Philip Johnson
Here is a quick interior sketch done to explain a rather complicated structural system. Contrast was achieved with crosshatching. The pens used to complete this illustration were three-, four-, and five-zero Rapidographs. The halftones were applied with a gray watercolor wash using a red sable brush.

This page, top
Pen and Ink
Two-ply Bristol Board
24 x 36 inches
Client: Gwathmey Siegel
Stippling and linework make this panorama work. The drawing layout was done from a photograph of a model. The color in the original was applied with Caran D'ache waterbase colored pencils after the drawing was complete.

Opposite, bottom
Pen and Ink
Two-ply Bristol Board
24 x 30 inches
Client: Robert Hillier Associates
A straight-line, eye-level perspective done from a mechanical layout. This is a rather stiff, disciplined illustration. The color in the original was applied with an airbrush. Notice the detail in the foliage and in the reflective glass.

39

Above
Pen and Ink
Two-ply Bristol Board
24 × 36 inches
Client: Robert Larsen Architect
The trees make this illustration truly believable. They were also the most time-consuming to draw.

Below, left
Pen and Ink
Two-ply Bristol Board
20 × 30 inches
Client: David Wachsman
These profile trees had to be simple or they would have hidden the building.

Below, right
Pen and Ink
Two-ply Bristol Board
30 × 30 inches
Client: John Carl Warnecke & Associates
This is another aerial view in which each tree was drawn with care. An effective drawing can never be rushed.

Opposite, top and center, left
Pen and Ink
Double-thick Illustration Board
24 x 36 inches
Client: Grozier Kearns & Phillipi
This freehand illustration was done from a combination of photographs—a photograph of the architect's model and a photograph of the actual site. The two were put to-

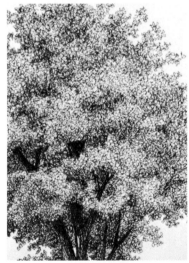

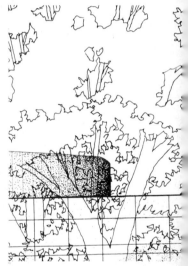

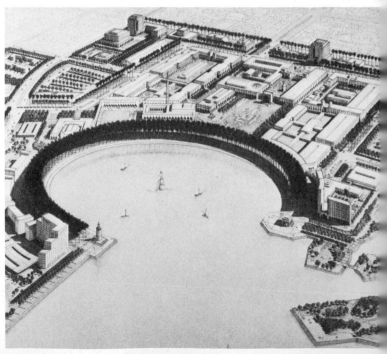

gether to form the layout. The drawing was then done in three- and four-zero Rapidographs. A watercolor wash was applied, and the colors were blended using a red sable brush.

Below, and right
Pen and Ink
Two-ply Bristol Board
24 × 36 inches
Client: Perkins and Will
Each palm tree took approximately twenty minutes to draw. This should give you an idea of the amount of time spent on this illustration.

Left
Pen and Ink
Double-thick Crescent Illustration Board;   30 × 40 inches
Client: John Carl Warnecke & Associates

Below
Pen and Ink
Two-ply Bristol Board
20 x 36 inches
Client: Lionel Coste, Architect
Trees and landscape were the most time-consuming elements of this drawing. Each tree took one hour or more to complete. The foreground is the most detailed area of all. The layout was done from a photograph of a model.

Bottom
Pen and Ink
Two-ply Bristol Board
24 x 36 inches
Client: The City of New York
Try drawing twenty or thirty thousand people—it will drive you insane! In order to make the Yankee Stadium renovation seem more realistic, these people had to be drawn. The drawing was completed using five- and six-zero Rapidographs.

Top
Pen and Ink
Two-ply Bristol Board
8 × 10 inches
Client: BBDO Advertising
Here are more examples of trees incorporating different scales and penpoints, but the same techniques.

Above, left
Pen and Ink
Two-ply Bristol Board
24 × 36 inches
Client: BBDO Advertising

Above
Pen and Ink
Double-thick Crescent Illustration
Board;   30 × 40 inches
Client: John Carl Warnecke &
Associates

5. PEOPLE

People and their surroundings (cars, stop signs, mailboxes, and so on) give illustrations the illusion of reality to the viewer. People lend scale to the illustration, enabling the viewer to judge size and distance. It is important, therefore, not only to draw the people accurately but to distribute them naturally throughout the illustration. Never bunch figures in the foreground so that they appear as if they are trying to escape from your illustration. When drawing figures do not have too many of them staring out at the viewer. They should not draw attention to themselves and should remain in character with the illustration. For example, three figures dressed in summer clothing and one with an overcoat on, or a girl in a bathing suit walking down a city street, would be inappropriate.

Clip files and clip books are a must. The *Illustration Guide* by Larry Evans (Van Nostrand Reinhold) is, I think, the best. It gives numerous examples of trees, cars, and people, done at various scales. The figures can be traced directly onto any illustration.

Eye-Level Perspectives

All of the figures on this page, the preceding page, and the following page have been traced onto these illustrations at eye level. See if you can find some of the characters in these illustrations in other illustrations in this book. Can you find Jackie Kennedy?

Page after next
Pen and Ink
Two-ply Bristol Board
15 × 26 inches
Client: Norman, Lawrence, Patterson and Farrell
Here is an illustration (originally in color) done for an ad agency, in which the figures are of critical importance; in fact, they *are* the illustration. I will give you a step-by-step description of how the drawing was done: First, a rough was done in color for position and style. Next, a precise ink outline drawing was made on tracing paper. Finally, the drawing was done on two-ply Bristol, using a three- and a four-zero Rapidgraph. The color was applied with watercolors, colored pencil, and airbrush.

47

BASF and American Textiles
A Working Combination

The BASF Wyandotte commitment to the American Textile Industry is hard at work. Over 500 BASF employees are producing textile dyes and auxiliaries in 2 fully modernized plants within quick delivery of most of the American textile processing industry. Our plants, located in Rensselaer, N.Y. and Charlotte, N.C. are producing our Palanil® and Palacet® disperse dyes, Bafixan® transfer dyes, Palanthrene® vat dyes, Acidol® and Vialon® acid dyes and Basacryl® basic dyes as well as an extensive line of processing auxiliaries.

Our ability to serve the American textile processing industry is assured both by our investment in modern plants as well as by our investment in the latest production equipment.

These investments in improved production are supported by modern warehousing and distribution systems to provide you with fast service as well as quality products.

When you work with BASF you not only get quality and service, you have available one of the most extensive technical capabilities in the industry. Our two laboratories are within easy reach, always ready to help and we maintain a high ratio of technical to sales personnel.

BASF Wyandotte Corporation
Textile Colors & Chemicals Dept.
100 Cherry Hill Rd., P.O. Box 181
Parsippany, N.J. 07054

Serving the American Textile Industry

BASF

6. ELEVATIONS— PLANS—SECTIONS

These are the drawings from which buildings are constructed. When presented as straightforward working drawings, they can be rather mundane and boring. However, these same drawings can become exciting and interesting when drawn with imagination. The manner in which shade and shadow are added, the reflective quality of glass, and the delineation of different materials, all give the drawing interest. Sometimes a drawing of this type must be done as part of a presentation, and you must know how to achieve a sense of reality and excitement in a minimum amount of time. I have always attempted, through the use of shade and shadow, to make the plan, section, or elevation appear to have depth. I think the look of any one of these drawings is definitely different from and sometimes more successful than that of a perspective. Judge for yourself.

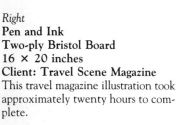

Right
Pen and Ink
Two-ply Bristol Board
16 × 20 inches
Client: Travel Scene Magazine
This travel magazine illustration took approximately twenty hours to complete.

Below, left
Pen and Ink
Two-ply Bristol Board
15 × 20 inches
Client: Charles Noyes
This is another very detailed outline illustration with no shade or shadow. The drawing was done using a four-zero Rapidograph.

Below, right and opposite
Pen and Ink
Two-ply Bristol Board
10 × 24 inches
Client: Discount Corporation of America
Here is an elevation drawn freehand and treated with stippling and line work. Notice that the glass has been left white. We felt that to have drawn reflection, or shade and shadow, would have been too much making the illustration appear overdone. How do you know when to stop working on a drawing, when to leave the glass white, or when to add linework? The answer to these questions is that this knowledge comes with experience, with critical examination of illustrations, and with making, and learning from, mistakes.

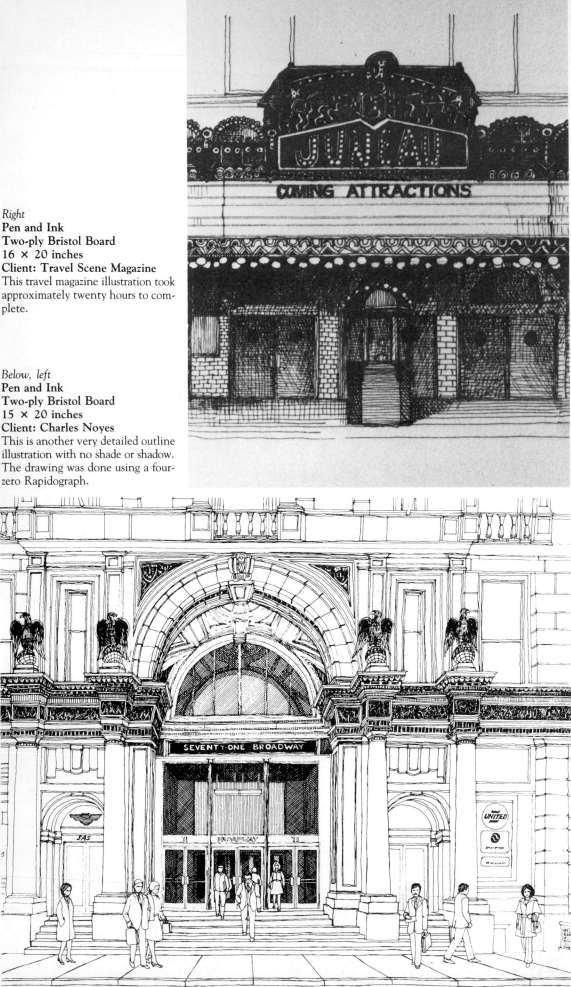

n and Ink
vo-ply Bristol Board
) × 30 inches
ient: Geller Design

is is yet another elevation per-
ective. However, in this drawing
e scale is very intimate. We see
ch brick and all the building or-
ment. The drawing was laid out
pencil first, from a series of slides,
e of which is shown. The first
ncil layout was very rough. From
s, another tracing paper overlay
s made to tighten the drawing

with respect to its detail and precision. The drawing was then traced
with a 2H pencil onto a piece of two-
ply Bristol board, kid finish. After it
was checked for accuracy, the drawing was completed with a three- and
four-zero Rapidograph pen. The
drawing was done completely freehand: the layout was done with a
straightedge, with great care and accuracy. Then the final drawing was
done very carefully over this layout
without instruments, using only a
pen. I find this method gives the

drawing a looseness and an infor-
mality not attainable using only
straight lines. The busy parts of the
drawing attract the viewer's eye,
making the rest of the drawing appear quiet by comparison. The important areas of the drawing are those
which have been drawn in detail.
Notice how the viewer's eye can be
moved around the illustrations
through either the abundance of
linework and detail, or the lack of
them.

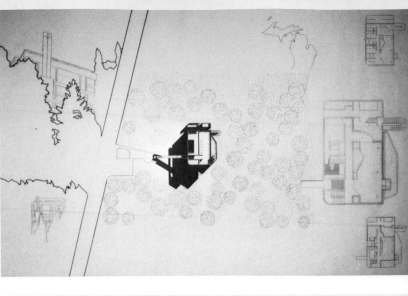

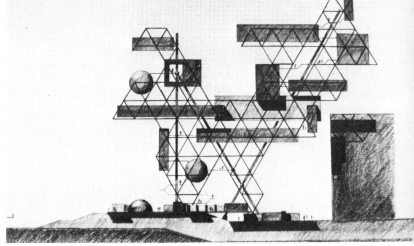

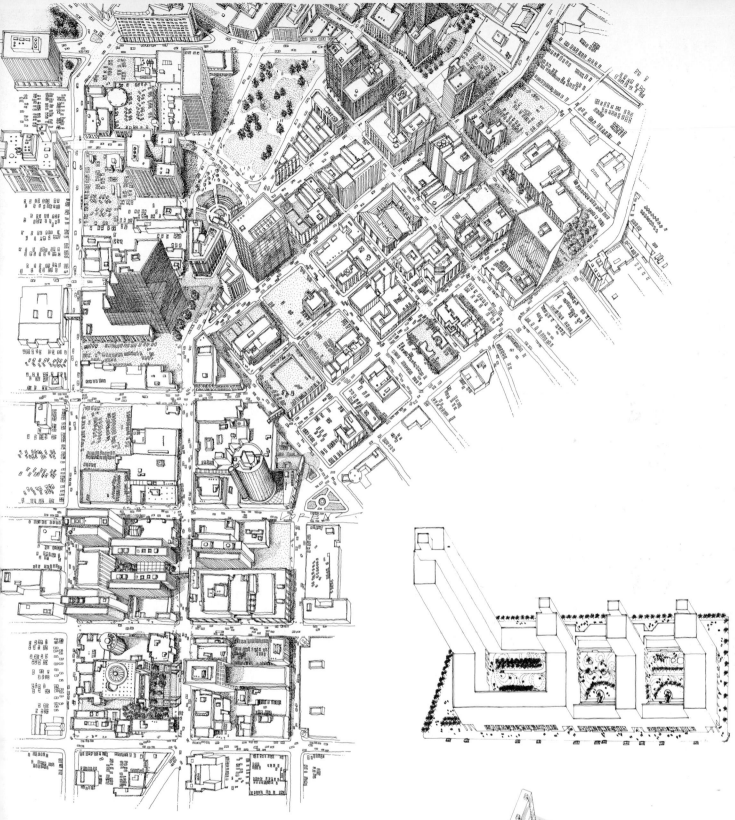

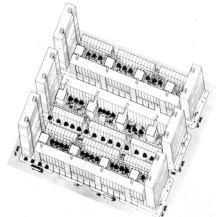

Student Drawings

The student drawings on this page and the facing page are successful for the same reason: they control your eye through the intelligent use of line and detail.

All of these drawings were done in pen and ink for Warren Gran, a New York architect. They are axonometrics and site plans. Notice the careful linework and the details.

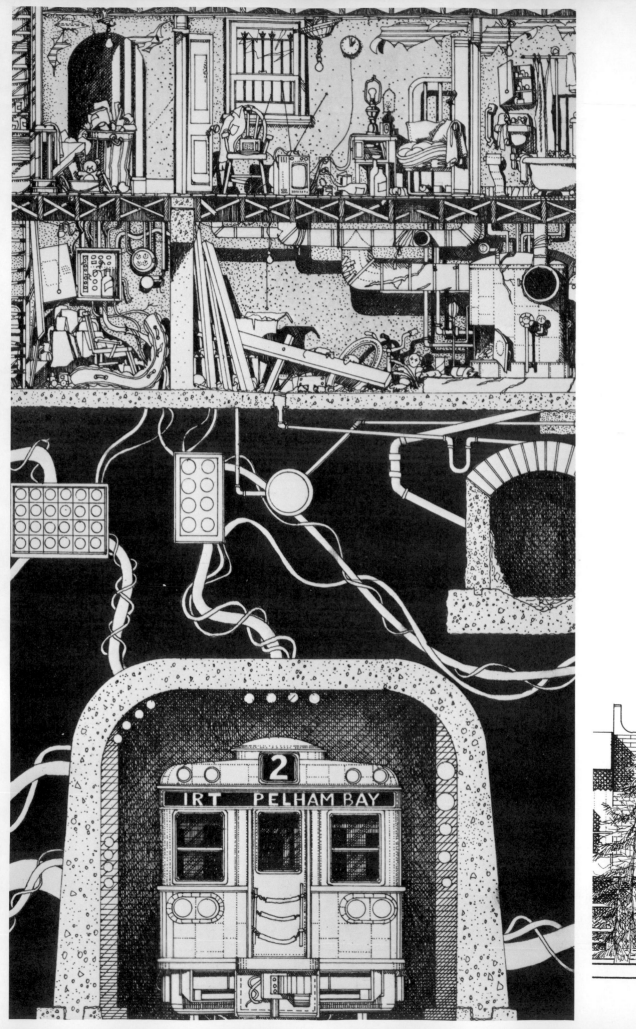
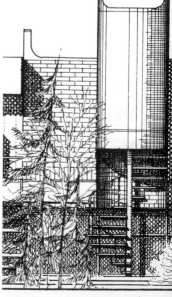

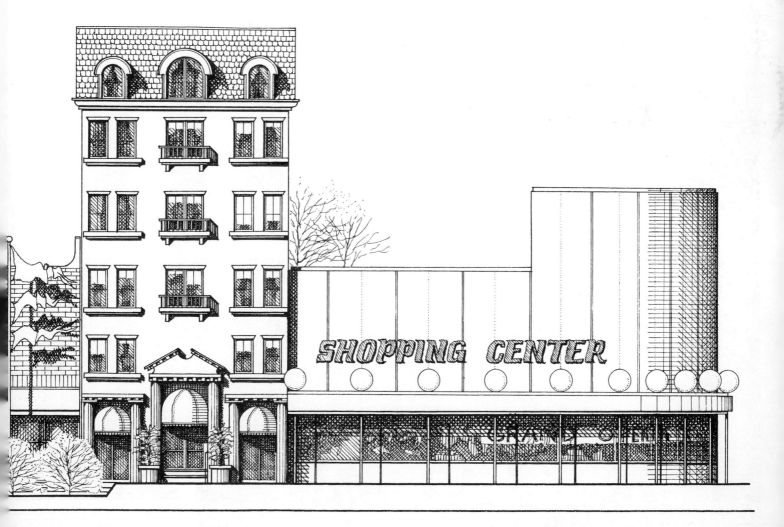

Below and opposite
Pen and Ink
Two-ply Bristol Board
20 × 30 inches
Client: Perkins and Will
These three drawings were done as one-point perspectives. All three are essentially elevation perspectives, meaning that the layout started with an elevation and was laid out mechanically from that. Once the elevation was translated into a perspective, the people were traced onto the layout. The drawings were then completed in ink using three- and four-zero Rapidograph pens.

Following Spread
Pen and Ink
Two-ply Bristol Board
20 × 30 inches
Client: Sidney Katz, FAIA

Pen and Ink
Two-ply Bristol Board
20 × 30 inches
Client: Sidney Katz, FAIA

Pen and Ink
Two-ply Bristol Board
20 × 30 inches
Client: Sidney Katz, FAIA
Each of these three freehand sketches was done in twenty hours or less. The importance of speed in illustration cannot be overemphasized. It seems there is always another deadline which is closer than the last. You must learn to develop a sketch quietly and accurately; the sketch must also elicit a positive response from the viewer.

7. METHODS OF PERSPECTIVE

I have always chosen the method of layout for any of my drawings with an eye towards simplicity and speed of execution. I almost always use the camera to produce my drawings, because it is the quickest and surest method. At times, however, I have to lay out a perspective using the mechanical layout method. I use the conventional method that can be understood by reading the following texts:

Ching, Frank. *Architectural Graphics*. New York: Van Nostrand Reinhold Company, 1975.

Coulin, Claudius. *Step-by-step Perspective*. New York: Van Nostrand Reinhold Company, 1971.

Forseth, Kevin. *Graphics for Architecture*. New York: Van Nostrand Reinhold Company, 1980.

Gill, Robert. *VNR Manual of Rendering with Pen and Ink*. New York: Van Nostrand Reinhold Company, 1984.

All of these books give very detailed explanations and diagrams of perspective methods. One method I use that is not included in any of the above texts and would, I think, be of some use in diagramming, is the "eyeball" sketch method shown in the following two pages. It allows me to set up a perspective, working solely with the human figure.

Diagram 1 Draw the figure, locating the horizon line at eye level.
Diagram 2 Locate the vanishing points.
Diagram 3 By eye, imagine and draw five foot by five foot squares.
Diagram 4 Draw the squares in both directions.
Diagrams 5 and 6 Using these squares, draw a grid on the ground, and vertically. You now have a framework within which you can draw your perspective.
Diagram 7 Overlay the framework, begin perspective.
Diagram 8 Finish perspective.

Always save the charts that you make, as you may be able to use them again. I recommend you purchase a set of Lawson Perspective Charts (Van Nostrand Reinhold). They use approximately the same method I have described and are preprinted and easy to use. As you will no doubt learn, there are almost an infinite number of methods of mechanical and chart perspective. You will come up with your own method in time. Remember, if it looks right, it is right, but it cannot be right unless it looks correct.

1

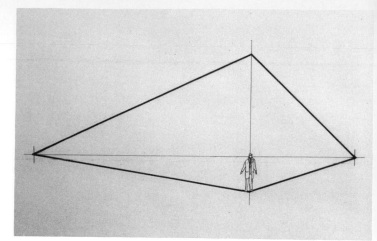

2

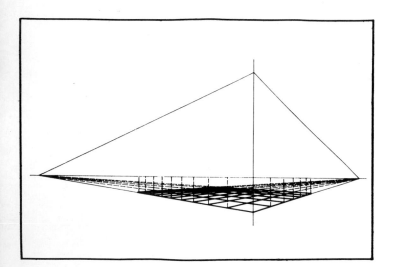

5

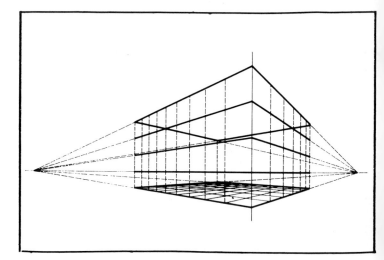

6

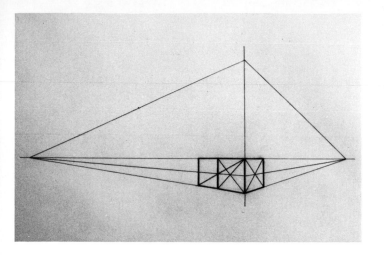

3

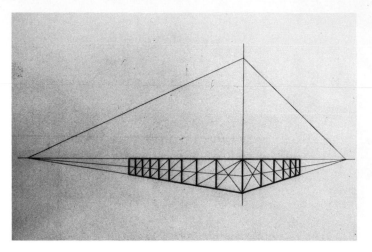

4

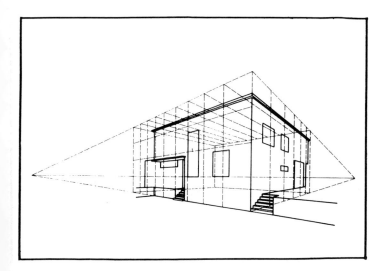

7

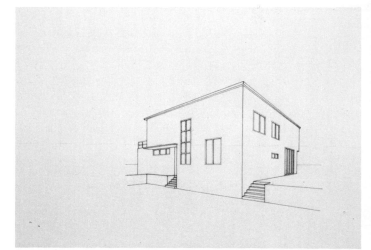

8

Right
Pen and Ink
Two-ply Bristol Board
24 × 20 inches
Client: Clark Harris Tribble and
Li

Below
Pen and Ink
Two-ply Bristol Board
20 × 30 inches
Client: M. Paul Friedberg

Left
Pen and Ink
Two-ply Bristol Board
20 × 30 inches
Client: Saul Silverman

Below
Pen and Ink
Two-ply Bristol Board
20 × 30 inches
Client: Clark Harris Tribble and Li
Here are some examples of perspectives done using the sketch technique. Each drawing was done in approximately eight hours. The layouts were done completely by eye, and each took approximately one hour to complete.

8. PLAN PERSPECTIVE—
SECTION PERSPECTIVE

These are very simple techniques I use to explain volumes. I start with a plan or a section and, using the sketch technique detailed in chapter 7, draw the volume of the room. Just imagine that you have removed the ceiling of a room and are looking down into it. This is what you will see with a plan perspective. If you were to take a wall from a building and look into it, that would be a section perspective. The five foot by five foot grid must be added in order to have a means of placing both furniture and architectural elements within the space.

Diagram 1,2 Begin with a plan; eyeball the squares coming up at you; Add five foot by five foot squares.

Diagram 3, 4, 5 Using the squares as a means to measure everything within the room, lay out furniture, materials, and other elements.

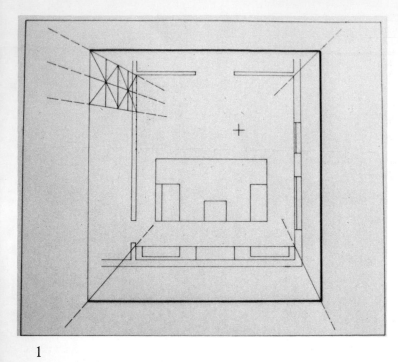

1

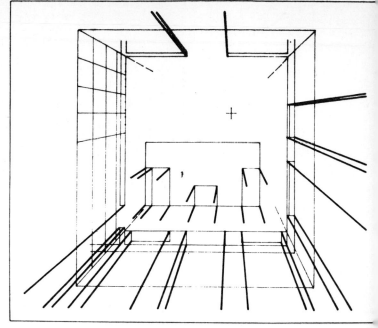

2

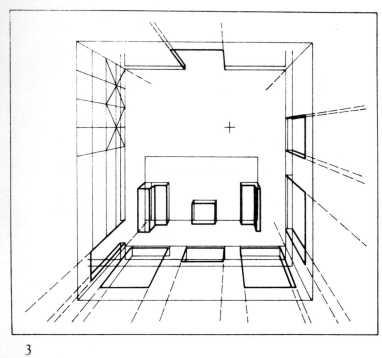

3

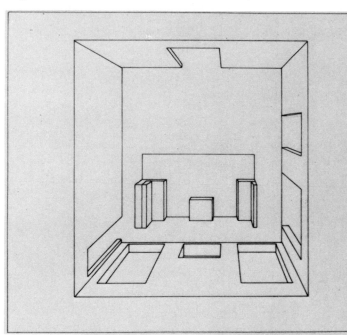

4

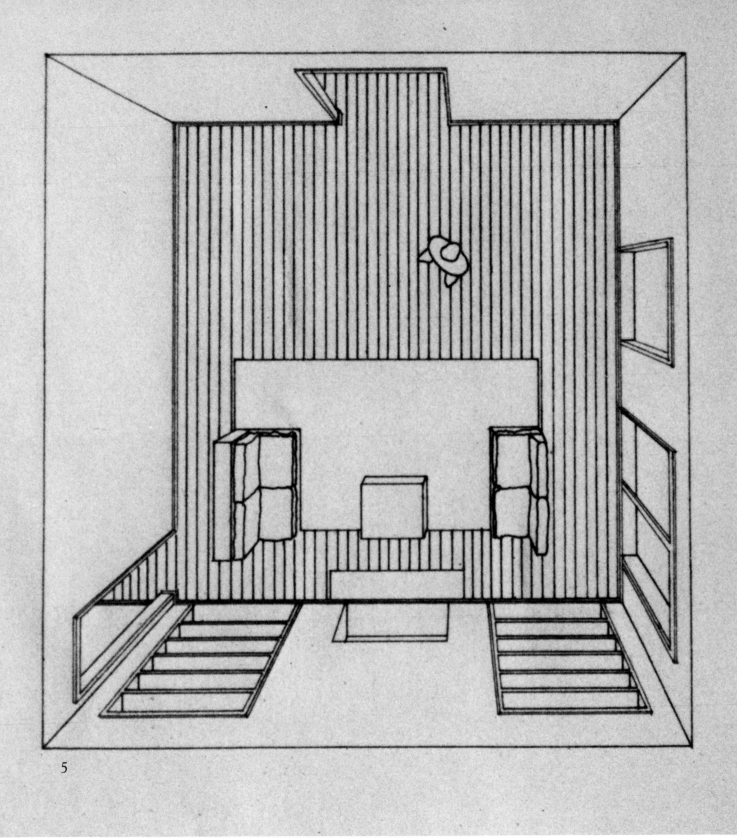

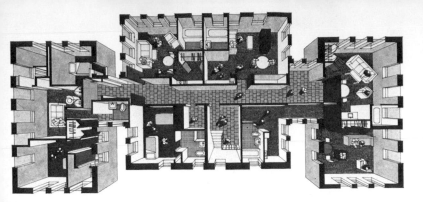

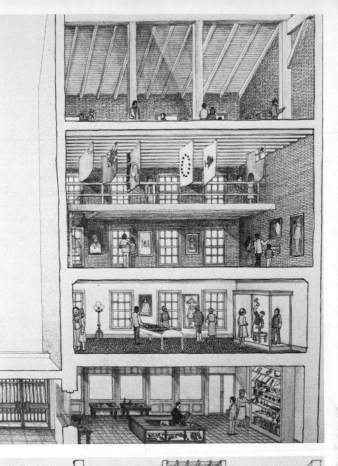

Opposite
Pen and Ink
Two-ply Bristol Board
24 x 36 inches
Client: Soskin and Thompson

Here is Rockefeller Center done as a section and plan perspective. This is one of the most interesting and successful drawings we have done recently, as well as being one of the most time-consuming. The layout was done from a combination of model photographs and site photographs. The drawing was done straight-line; the colors in the original were applied using pencil, watercolor, and airbrush.

Above
Pen and Ink
Double-thick Crescent Illustration
Board;   20 × 40 inches
Client: Frost Associates

Below and right
Pen and Ink
Double-thick Crescent Illustration
Board;   20 × 30 inches
Client: Fraunces Tavern

Below
Pen and Ink
Double-thick Crescent Illustration
Board;   20 × 30 inches
Client: Warren Gran Associates
All of these drawings were done in
pen and ink, using three-, four-, and
five-zero Rapidographs. These are
section perspectives and, as such,
explain the interior space—the materials, trees, and plants—as no other
type of drawing could. For this project, a section perspective was the
easiest and most direct way to in-
dicate the character of the building
as well as the level changes. As you
can see from the detail, these drawings are extremely accurate even
though they were done freehand.
Each drawing took approximately
sixty hours to complete.

Right and opposite
Pen and Ink
Double-thick Crescent Illustration
Board;   20 × 30 inches
Client: Edward L. Barnes

9. PHOTOGRAPHIC PERSPECTIVE

Imagine a layout method in which some magical tool does all the work for you. The method exists, and the magical tool is simply a camera. You may do the layout in either of two ways. The first method involves taking a slide with your camera and projecting the slide onto a piece of tracing paper, using a slide projector. The second method is similar. Take a picture, make a print, and trace that. I find the slide method easier, because I can make the image any size I want simply by moving the projector forward or backward. Always use Ektachrome film when working with slides, since it can be processed in a matter of hours. When transferring from slide to paper, make sure you turn the slide off every fifteen minutes or so, since the projector gets so hot it might actually burn or warp the slide. Whenever doing a photographic layout try to make more than one slide of the photograph you are using, just in case the worst happens. Transfer as much detail as possible from the slide, since that will save you guesswork later on.

In the following drawings, originally in color, the layout was done by building a simple model, photographing it with slide film, and projecting the image. I always project and draw the image on tracing paper first, since there are inevitably visual and technical corrections that must be made before the image is transferred to illustration board. Both drawings were done in pen and ink first, using three-, four-, and five-zero Rapidograph pens. The color was then added with brush and colored pencil.

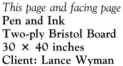

This page and facing page
Pen and Ink
Two-ply Bristol Board
30 × 40 inches
Client: Lance Wyman
The cardinal rule in laying out perspectives is: *the best way is always the fastest way.* Photographic perspective allows you to build a perspective using photographs or slides; the camera does all of the work. In this particular drawing, I began by photographing an architectural model, using a "fisheye" (14 mm. wide-angle) lens, which curves and distorts all parallel lines. I then set up a curving grid and drew the surrounding buildings. The original photograph of the model had the most vivid color, so the surrounding buildings were drawn less vividly so as not to distract the viewer's eye. The color was done with watercolor and airbrush. The sky and clouds were done by spraying first with airbrush and then blotting the spray with cotton and a mixture of bleach and water in a ratio of 1 part bleach to four parts water. To make this trick work, you must use either Luma or Dr. Martin's watercolor dyes. The bleach will erase the color, making the remaining white areas look like clouds.

Above
Pen and Ink
Double-thick Crescent Illustration
Board;   30 × 40 inches
Client: Lionel Coste
The model for this building was
minimal: just boxes, with the elevations glued to them with rubber
cement. The trees took the most
time. They are also what give a feeling of reality to the drawing.

Opposite, bottom, and left
Pen and Ink
Two-ply Bristol Board
20 × 30 inches
Client: Clark Harris Tribble and
Li
The model was built right on top of
the site plan which allowed us to find
contours easily. In this drawing, although color was used minimally,
the slight gray tone on our building
is extremely important, since it at-
tracts the viewer's eye.

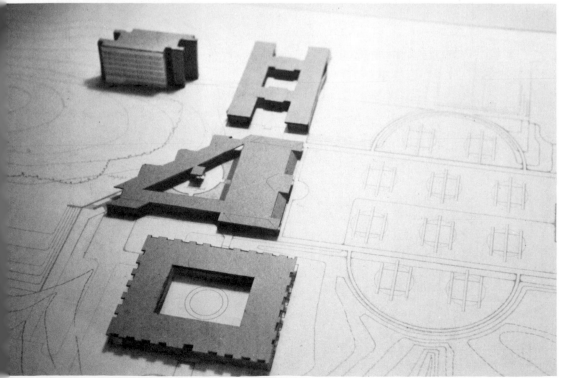

Here are three projects, all
done using my camera (loaded
with Kodak Ektachrome film)
and the slide projector as a
means to project the images.

This page, top and center
Pen and Ink
Two-ply Bristol Board
30 × 30 inches
Client: Warren Gran Associates

Working with the architect's model
this layout was simple. The model
merely had to be photographed and
then projected and drawn on illustration board. Once projected in
pencil, though, the drawing itself
was rather complex. The architect
wanted the illustration to be done as
though it were evening, allowing the
viewer to see both the exterior and
the interior of the building. The glow
from the interior lighting gives a
warm feeling to the building. A
nighttime illustration is always more
difficult because it requires not only
more work, but some delicate airbrushing. You must finish the drawing as if it were daytime and then
"bring on" the night. There is always
the danger of spraying on a little too
much night and ruining the entire
drawing. I sprayed around the building with a dark blue-gray, while still
leaving a delicate glow around the
building. I then went over this glow
lightly with both a white pencil and
a yellow-white Prismacolor pencil, to
reinforce the light areas.

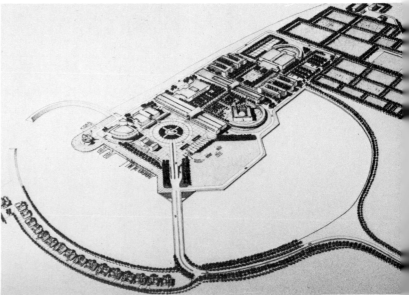

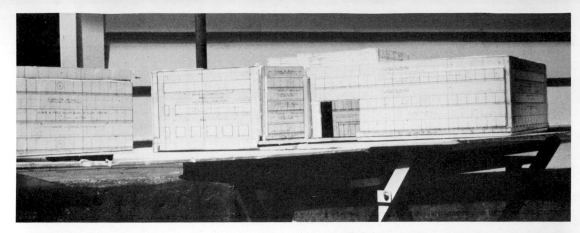

Right
Pen and Ink
Two-ply Bristol Board
20 × 30 inches
Client: Bond-Ryder
Here is a model constructed of cardboard, with the elevations rubbercemented to them. This made the location of windows, doors, and all architectural details a rather simple chore. The drawing itself was done in Rapidograph, with the color being applied later.

Opposite bottom
Pen and Ink
Two-ply Bristol Board
30 × 40 inches
Client: John Carl Warnecke & Associates
Here is an illustration that we did directly from a slide taken of the site plan. Constructing this aerial perspective from the architectural drawing would have been nearly impossible because the scale of this group of buildings is so immense. By using the camera we were given our layout, but not heights. This was done by estimation.

10. ERASING, CUTTING IN, MAKING CHANGES

Working in pen and ink is an exact and indelible kind of illustration, yet mistakes are inevitable. What happens when you make a mistake? Corrections are simple if you follow certain procedures:

Always work on 100 percent rag illustration board or paper. This is top-quality paper and will allow erasure more easily. Whenever you have to erase an ink line, try to mar as small an area as possible. After erasing, smear a little graphite over the newly erased area. When you are ready to redraw your line, draw over this graphite area and your line will not feather or spread. Once the ink is dry, erase the graphite and you will never notice the erasure.

After erasing with an ink eraser, remember that you have changed the surface of the board. If you try to apply a watercolor wash, the color will be darker and you will be able to see the erased area. Therefore you must apply a much lighter wash, knowing it will get darker. Always work on a medium-rough surface.

Never be bothered by mistakes, unless you repeat them.

This next job, shown on the following page, is an example of a change made without erasure. As you can see, the two illustrations are identical with the exception of the skylight in the top illustration. The originals were done on two-ply Bristol board. To remove the skylight I cut along the roof line. I then cut another piece of two-ply and rubber cemented it back into this space. The seam is hidden along the ink line of the roof. The only way that you would know of this change would be to run your finger along the seam. Since most of my work is done for photographic reproduction, this kind of change presents no problem.

Right

Right
Pen and Ink
Two-ply Bristol Board
24 × 36 inches
Client: Gruzen & Partners
The sky and reflection are very important to this drawing's success. The clouds were done by crosshatching with a very fine crow quill pen in black ink and washing the color over these lines with a brush. The reflections are simply horizontal lines. The tone of the reflection can be changed by changing the spacing of the lines.

Below
Pen and Ink
Double-thick Crescent Illustration Board;   24 × 36 inches
Client: Robert Hillier
This drawing, originally in color, took about forty hours to produce. The drawing layout was done by taking a slide of a model and projecting it onto a piece of Crescent illustration board. The color was done using Caran D'ache water-soluble pencils. The background and sky were done with airbrush.

11. AERIAL TECHNIQUE

There are several general points to consider whenever undertaking an aerial drawing:

1. You must have excellent information. You need the *latest* photographs, slides, and maps from as many different angles as possible. You can never have too much information.
2. Design the illustration in your mind. What will it look like? Who is going to use your illustration? What kind of feeling should it have? Should it be cartoon-like, realistic, playful, serious?
3. Choose your media. Is it black-and-white or color, pencil or pen-and-ink?
4. Bear in mind how much time you have to complete the drawing. This will determine the size of the illustration.
5. Decide on a layout method. Are you working from photographs or slides, or are you building your own perspective?

You are now ready to begin. Remember that aerial drawings take longer to complete than any other type of drawing, so charge accordingly.

Next spread
Pen and Ink
Two-Ply Bristol Board
16 × 20 inches
Client: Doremus Advertising

This job was done for an advertising agency that planned a campaign of four magazine advertisements. The idea was to get closer and closer to the building in each drawing. The interesting thing about this job is that each drawing was done using a different layout method.

1) We began with a black-and-white photograph of Manhattan. This was traced onto Albanene tracing paper. This was then overlayed and the Bank of New York building was added. These two layouts were traced onto a two-ply Bristol board, kid finish. Using a 2H pencil, the drawing was inked using three- and four-zero Rapidograph pens. Color was added with brush and water-soluble pencil.

2) A slide was projected onto a piece of tracing paper. All of the buildings were drawn precisely from this projection with the exception of the Bank of New York building. This was drawn on a separate piece of tracing paper. The size was exaggerated, but not the detail. The finished drawing was done on the same board with the same pens as before.

3) This layout was completely made up and has no basis in reality. The buildings were moved around slightly, so as to make our building prominent. Again, the building size was exaggerated, not the detail.

4) The close-up of the building was done entirely from slides taken at the site. Each shot overlapped the one before it, which is almost like using a wide-angle lens. A wide-angle lens was not actually used because of the amount of distortion it produces when photographing at close distances. By using a regular lens and overlapping you eliminate much of the distortion. To complete the drawing, we made an 8 1/2 by 11 inch color Xerox of each and pieced them together for the layout. Once they were pieced and glued together, we traced them and transferred this drawing to a piece of two-ply Bristol board and, as before, drew them in pen and ink.

experience

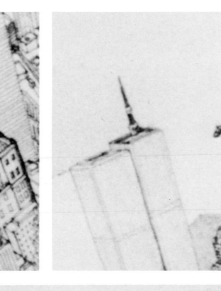

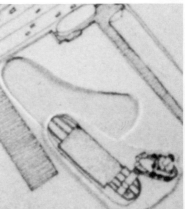

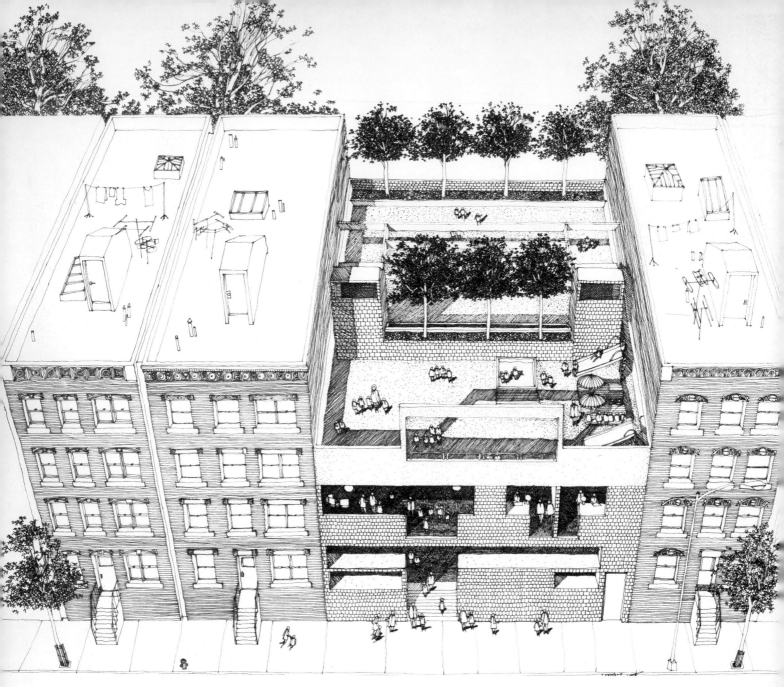

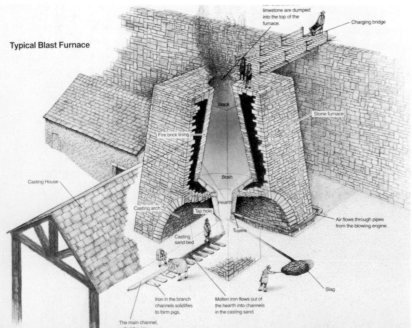

Typical Blast Furnace

limestone are dumped into the top of the furnace.

Charging bridge

Stack

Fire brick lining

Stone furnace

Casting House

Bosh

Hearth

Casting arch

Tap hole

Air flows through pipes from the blowing engine.

Casting sand bed

Tuyère

Iron in the branch channels solidifies to form pigs.

Molten iron flows out of the hearth into channels in the casting sand.

Slag

The main channel, called the sow

Below
Pen and Ink
Double-thick Crescent Illustration Board;   24 × 36 inches
Client: Pratt Institute
Whenever doing nighttime illustration remember to begin by treating the illustration as if it were daytime, using a shade side and sun side, even though there is no such thing. Once you have finished these values, you must add to them. You must envision a light source inside the building. There is a glow around each window and the light diminishes as the distance from the window increases. The colors are added as before; brush colors first, then pencil, then airbrush. Lastly, with night illustrations, I always add some white and pale-yellow colored pencil to give a feeling of the glow within a building and to indicate the direction of light.

Opposite, top
Pen and Ink
Two-ply Bristol Board
24 × 36 inches
Client: Clark Harris Tribble and Li Architects
The color in this illustration is a combination of watercolor wash and colored pencil. Always apply the watercolor wash first and then apply the pencil to highlight the wash. Make sure that the wash is dry first!

Opposite, bottom
Pen and Ink
Two-ply Bristol Board
24 × 36 inches
Client: Clark Harris Tribble and Li Architects
This is really just a black-and-white illustration, treated like a coloring book. Watercolors were applied to people, vegetables, signs, and the like. Some white pencil and colored pencils were applied to indicate the light source. This illustration sets a happy, bouncy, mood. It really does not tell much of an architectural story, but this was intentional.

12. MULTI-PHOTO TECHNIQUE

Sometimes, for one reason or another, you would rather not project a slide to complete a layout. For instance, if you have to use more than one slide to complete a layout this method is unfeasible. The easy method in such a case is as follows: First, overlap your slides so that when joined together, they make one big picture with no pieces missing. Next, make a Xerox reproduction (8½ by 11 inches) from each slide. This can be done inexpensively anywhere that photocopies are made. Then cut and glue these reproductions together to make one large image. Transfer this image onto tracing paper; trace it. Finally, photostat your drawing to size and the layout is done. The reason I do not advise photostatting the Xerox to size is that the image will not be sharp enough.

This page, top
Pen and Ink
Two-ply Bristol Board
30 × 40 inches
Client: HOK Architects
Two eye-level photographs were used to build this perspective. How could two photographs be put together to produce this drawing, when one photograph was taken at human scale in Lake Placid and the other one of a model in the architect's office? The answer is the use of the common denominator—the eye level of a human being. I photo-graphed the site at Lake Placid while standing on the ground. I then measured the distance from the ground to the lens of my camera. When photographing the model, I made sure my lens was the same distance above ground level and the same distance from the site, *but* in the same scale as the model. This gave me two photographs in the form of slides, both taken from the same distance and the same eye level. By doing this, I was able to put the two photographs together to produce the drawing.

Opposite, bottom
Pen and Ink
Two-ply Bristol Board
20 × 30 inches
**Client: John Carl Warnecke &
Associates**
This is a rather simple aerial, done
with a mechanical layout. The
drawing, originally in color, took
about thirty hours. Colors were done
with watercolor and water-soluble
pencil.

Left
Watercolor
**Double-thick Crescent Watercolor
Board;   16 × 24 inches**
Client: Diner's Club Magazine
The original of this illustration was
done entirely with natural-pigment
watercolor (Windsor Newton). A
very detailed pencil drawing using a
2H pencil was done first. The watercolor was applied directly over the
pencil. Once the watercolor was dry,
the pencil was erased with a white
plastic eraser.

Left and below
Pen and Ink
**Double-thick Crescent Illustration
Board;   24 × 36 inches**
Client: Perkins & Will
In this dramatically lit interior, the
larger areas of color were done with
airbrush. Smaller areas were done
using watercolor and brush. The entire illustration was done using a
straightedge.

Above and opposite
Pen and Ink
Double-thick Crescent Illustration Board; 24 × 36 inches
Client: Clark Harris Tribble and Li
I think this drawing will help make my method of applying color understandable. After the layout was done, the drawing was completed in black-and-white, and all shade and shadow textures were drawn in black-and-white, we were ready to apply the color. We first did the people in subdued colors; nothing that would bounce off the page; nothing that would take the viewer's eye from the architecture. Always sample the colors you are going to use *before* you use them. Once we finished the people, we added the trees and plants, using several greens. We applied flat tones first, without yet worrying about highlight, shades, or direction of light. Once all the colors were dry, we were ready to work with light. Usually we apply colored pencil, whites, and off-whites (yellows). We apply these colors in order to give light a direction, to give the light source a glow, and generally to add drama to the interior. I think if you study the drawing and the close-ups, the method of application becomes evident.

13. COLOR

The technique I use to do a color illustration is simple: It is the coloring-book technique. I begin by treating every drawing as a black-and-white drawing. Once I am satisfied that I have a good black-and-white illustration, I am ready to apply color. Since the ink drawing is waterproof, there are no problems with smearing. I follow a simple system for the application of color:

The sky is usually done with airbrush and Luma dyes. I can then apply laundry bleach and water to the sky with a piece of cotton in order to produce the clouds. Once this is done and has been allowed to dry, I immediately apply fixative. When this has dried, I apply Prismacolor pencil, using yellows and whites for highlights.

Trees are colored using a brush and Luma dyes. The first wash is done in light tones and allowed to dry. This is followed by another application of the same tones. I then switch to Caran D'ache water-soluble pencils for highlights and shade leaves. Once the pencil is on the drawing, I apply a thin wash of water. This will turn the colors much darker; if I think a given color is too dark, I simply erase it lightly and the color lightens. Finally, the branches are colored with Pelikan inks—the brown tones are the best.

The buildings are done by mixing all of the above media, depending on the result desired. Always brush on a light wash before applying colored pencil; otherwise the texture of the board will read through as white spots. These rules, of course, are rather general. Take a careful look at the following drawings to note the results.

Following spread

Top
Pen and Ink
Double-thick Crescent Illustration Board
24 × 36 inches
Client: Fraunces Tavern

Bottom
Pen and Ink
Double-thick Crescent Illustration Board
24 × 36 inches
Client: John Carl Warnecke & Associates
Both of these drawings were done using my two-step method. First, they were drawn in pen and ink. Second, the color was added. The color here was done with watercolor, colored pencil, and airbrush. First a color sample—a discarded piece of the illustration board on which the final illustration was to be done—was used to sample all colors, in order to make sure they would appear the way I wanted them to on the final illustration. All color judgments were made from this piece of board. I then chose the colors that were most suitable for the illustration from a range of colored pencils, watercolors, and dyes. These were then applied either by brush or by hand. No permanent (oil base) markers were used, since they are not erasable and tend to bleed by capillary action through the illustration board. Once the colors were applied, I worked over them and blended them until I was satisfied that the coloring was right. After this had been completed, I was ready to apply the airbrush colors. This is always done last, since the airbrush colors must be sprayed with fixative as soon as they have been applied. The airbrush colors are also extremely delicate and can even be disturbed by the moisture in the artist's fingers or a drop of water. Once the airbrushing was finished, I was ready to apply a spray fixative. This is usually done from a distance of about twenty-four inches, so that the spray does not drip on the board. Always be aware that the fixative spray will darken most colors, especially airbrush colors. Be careful! Always experiment first, so that you are aware of the final result before you put any color down on the final illustration.

Opposite
Pen and Ink
Two-ply Bristol Board
24 × 36 inches
Client: Young & Rubicam

Bottom
Pen and Ink
Two-ply Bristol Board
24 × 36 inches
Client: Perkins and Will
Here is a layout done using the Lawson Perspective Charts. These charts are excellent for interiors. They give the illustrator a one foot by one foot grid on ceiling, floor, and walls. It is quite easy to put a perspective together using these charts, the only drawback being that they are simply not big enough for exteriors. Otherwise, they are a great time saver.

Top, right
Pen and Ink
Double-thick Crescent Illustration Board
30 × 40 inches
Client: City of New York
In order to show the whole neighborhood, the entire ballpark, and its relationship to parking facilities and surrounding highways, an aerial perspective had to be done. The layout was done by taking a slide from a helicopter and using this image as a basis. This initial image, of course, was added to, as new buildings, highways, and parking structures had been planned, but to produce a layout any other way would have been insanity.

Right
Pen and Ink
Double-thick Crescent Illustration Board
30 × 40 inches
Client: John Carl Warnecke & Associates
The layout was done by photographing a site plan. The photograph, in the form of a slide, was then projected onto a piece of tracing paper and all details were drawn. From this layout, the final drawing was done. The illustration took approximately sixty hours. Aerial drawings are always the most time-consuming, since they cover the largest paper surface and contain the most linework. It is for this reason that they are also the most expensive. Personally, I feel aerial perspectives are the most difficult drawings for the average viewer to understand, since the human figure is so small. I believe people relate to objects and figures they see in an illustration the same way they do in life. For this reason, I believe eye-level illustrations and sketches are usually preferable.

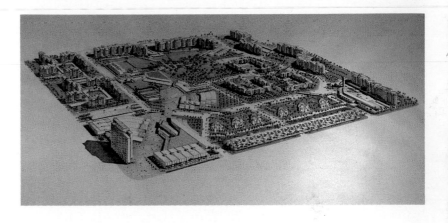

14. TEXTURES

Crosshatching, dotted lines, stippling, and combining gray ink and black ink, all produce one thing—texture. Drawing in pen and ink does not produce ultrarealistic illustration, and clients do not buy my illustrations for their realism. They buy them for a charm which pen and ink can produce. The ability to produce a texture comes with understanding the variables that go along with pen-and-ink work. The change in pen sizes, the quality of the line itself, and the blackness of the ink are the input. The output is the texture produced by this combination.

Pen and Ink
Two-ply Bristol Board
20 × 30 inches
Client: Middleburg-Middleton
Advertising
The textures of grass, trees, shingles, and water make this drawing work. The drawing is busy but busy with a purpose: it conveys the quiet even feeling of the countryside. This drawing was to be printed in a newspaper. It was important to create all of the textures, the light, shade, and shadow, entirely with linework. Washes and halftones do not print evenly in newspaper reproduction.

en and Ink
wo-ply Bristol Board
0 × 30 inches
lient: Middleburg-Middleton
dvertising

he second in the series, this draw-
g was done from a twenty-foot eye
vel, as opposed to the first drawing,
hich was done from a five-foot lev-
. Notice how the background fades
rough the gradation of the stip-
ing. The linework in the fore-
ound is always more pronounced
d heavier. This is another method
 making the perspective under-
ood.

15. CHARTS

Charts are a real time saver, especially for interior perspectives. A chart is a preprinted grid which allows you to locate vanishing points and measure horizontally. Once you are able to use the printed charts and understand them, it is an easy matter to begin to produce your own charts. I find these charts very accurate for small-scale (any building or space that is between fifty and sixty feet in width and length) drawings but really impossible to use on a large-scale project.

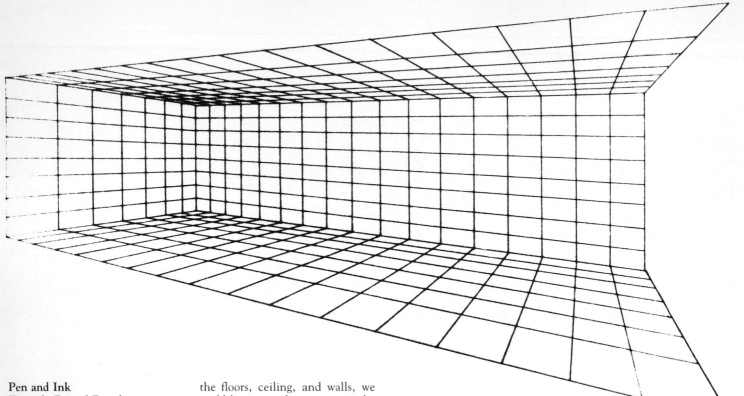

Pen and Ink
Two-ply Bristol Board
20 × 30 inches
Client: LCP Interiors
These layouts were both done using a perspective grid. This is, of course, the same method that the Lawson Perspective Charts employ. By using a one foot by one foot grid drawn on the floors, ceiling, and walls, we could be extremely accurate in the location of all architectural elements, such as furniture, windows, and doors. The textures were done in pen and ink using three- and four-zero Rapidographs. The drawings took approximately thirty-five hours each to complete.

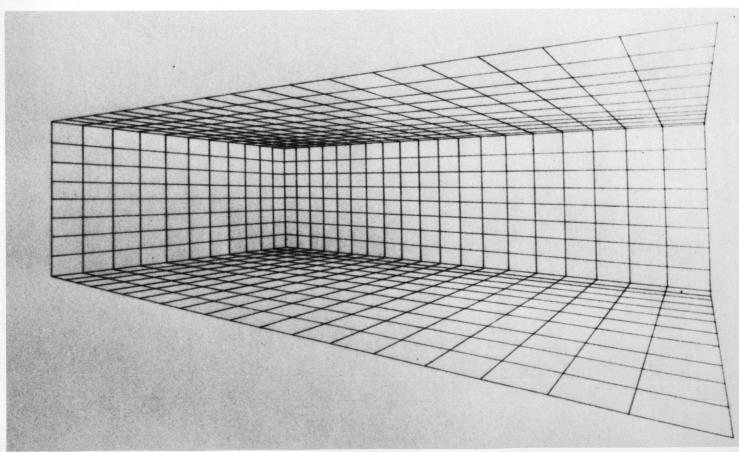

Pen and Ink
Double-thick Crescent Illustration Board;   20 × 30 inches
Client: Albert Lorenz
Being able to imitate textures to de-lineate the quality of light, shade, and shadow is what an illustration is really all about. A brick must look like a brick; a tree must look like a tree. Working from photographs may seem a simple task, but it really is not. A close examination of both the photograph and the drawing will in-dicate the method of imitating tex-ture, shade, and shadow. The tex-tures and the feeling of the linework change as the choice of pen points changes. Observe the line. Is it a solid line, or a dotted line? Notice, too, the texture. What kind of tex-ture do you see, and how was it done?

Pen and Ink
Double-thick Crescent Illustration
Board;   20 × 40 inches
Client: Commodities Exchange
Action in illustrations is a must.
Never let an illustration appear dull
or static. Have your people appear
lively, as if they are enjoying being
a part of your illustrations.

16. PHOTO-DRAWING MONTAGE

Another technique I find very successful is the incorporation of a photograph with a drawing in such a way that the two work together. You must always begin with the photograph; it gives you vanishing points and an eye level. Once these are established you may begin the drawing. I do the first rough on tracing paper, making sure that the photograph and my rough work well together. I then complete the drawing on 100 percent rag board or paper, in pen and ink, with or without color. Lastly, I glue in the photo. Once this is done I usually photograph the montage and present this as the final product, since there are no seams.

I like to use this method of drawing because it simplifies my task. The photograph establishes both the scale and the viewpoint and gives me the direction of light. Ideally, the viewer will realize that the finished product is a montage but will not be disturbed by this fact.

Pen and Ink
Two-ply Bristol Board
24 × 36 inches
Client: Lance Wyman Associates
This illustration began by photographing a very detailed architectural model. To show the interior we had to invent a grid. To begin the grid we used the floor-to-floor dimension, which we knew to be ten feet. The vanishing points were given to us by the photograph itself. The grid was set up just as in the section perspective method. The final drawing was done on a piece of two-ply Bristol board and then pasted onto the photograph. A photograph of this composite was then taken so that there were no seams, and the job was done. This drawing took about forty-five hours.

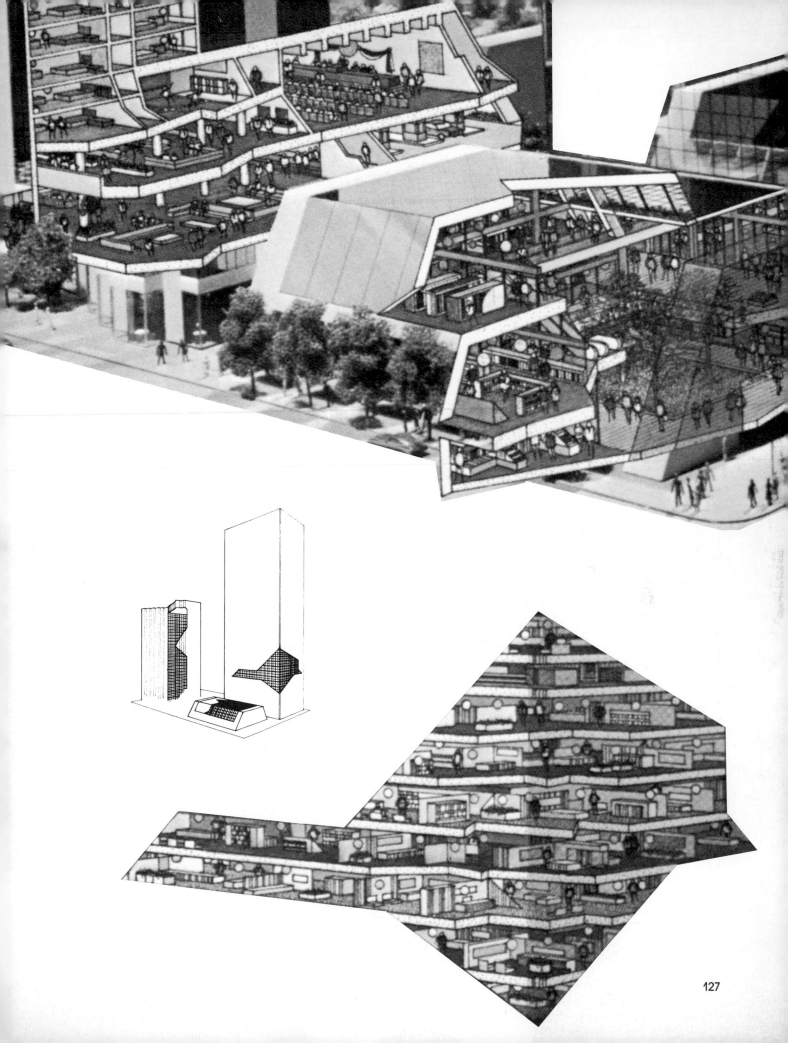

Pen and Ink
Two-ply Bristol Board
20 × 30 inches
Client: Albert Lorenz
Here is a promotional illustration. This drawing was done mainly to announce the fact that I was moving my studio from Brooklyn to Long Island. It was also done as a self-promotional example of my illustration technique. Freelance illustrators must keep their work in the public eye constantly in order to get more work. This drawing was done entirely in pen and ink with three-zero Rapidographs. It took about one hundred hours to complete.

Opposite
Pen and Ink
Two-ply Bristol Board
20 × 30 inches
Client: Albert Lorenz

Pen and Ink
Two-ply Bristol Board
20 × 36 inches
Client: Max Urbahn and Associates

Pen and Ink
Two-ply Bristol Board
18 × 24 inches
Client: Perkins and Will Associates

Pen and Ink
Two-ply Bristol Board
24 × 36 inches
Client: Armand Bartos Associates

Left
Pen and Ink
Two-ply Bristol Board
20 × 24 inches
Client: Clark Harris Tribble and Li

Below, left
Pen and Ink
Two-ply Bristol Board
20 × 36 inches
Client: Gwathmey Siegel

Below, right
Pen and Ink
Two-ply Bristol Board
20 × 30 inches
Client: Rogers Butler and Bergun Architects

Each one of these drawings was laid out mechanically. Each then went its own way. I think it is very important to see the difference that can be made in a drawing through the manner in which a line or tree is drawn. Each of these drawings, with the exception of the sketches, took forty hours to complete. The ability to judge how long an illustration will take to finish is important. The ability comes with practice; after having done a few illustrations, I am sure you will start to develop a very accurate sense of your own drawing time. It is this accurate sense of personal drawing time which marks the professional.

This page and opposite

Pen and Ink
Double-thick Crescent Illustration
Board;   30 × 40 inches
Client: Austin Kelley Advertising

Two hundred hours! That is how long this illustration took to complete. Stippling was the only drawing method, as far as I was concerned, that would show the scale and the interest of this vast site. Note the care and accuracy of the stippling in delineating the trees. This is a technique that cannot be rushed, I am sorry to say.

Following spread
Pen and Ink
Double-thick Crescent Illustration
Board; 20 × 30 inches
Client: John O'Neill

Pen and Ink
Double-thick Crescent Illustration
Board; 24 × 36 inches
Client: David Hirsch

Pen and Ink
Double-thick Crescent Illustration
Board; 20 × 30 inches
Client: Bond-Ryder

Pen and Ink
Double-thick Crescent Illustration
Board; 24 × 36 inches
Client: Lionel Coste

Pen and Ink
Double-thick Crescent Illustration
Board; 24 × 36 inches
Client: Sidney Katz

Pen and Ink
Double-thick Crescent Illustration
Board; 20 × 30 inches
Client: Richard Farley

These drawings share precisely delineated textures and carefully drawn linework. All of the drawings were done using the Lawson Perspective Charts. We had to make some slight modifications on the charts to use them on exteriors, since they are really designed for interior or smaller spaces. The modification is simple—just double or triple the scale of the chart, and proceed from there.

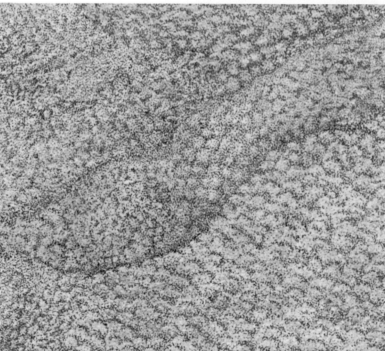

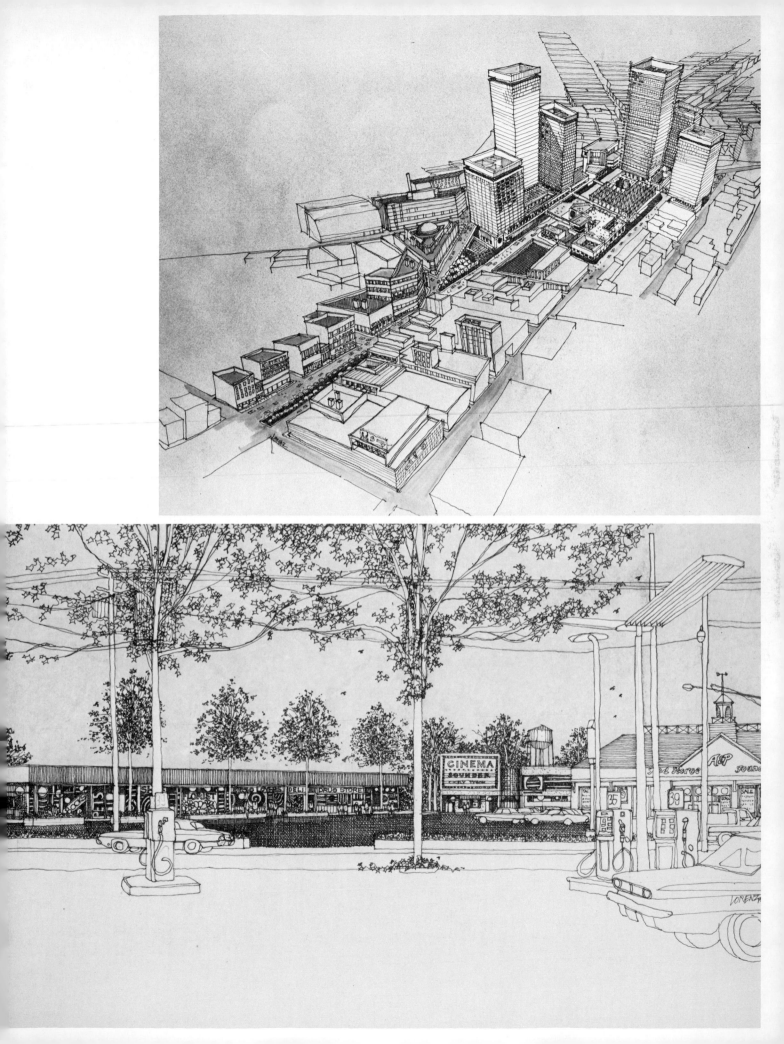

17. CARTOONS

Every drawing has a character of its own, be it serious, informative, or playful. A cartoon-type drawing can be great fun to look at and be a very successful drawing at the same time. The fact that a drawing is cartoon-like does not lessen the work or care involved; the only characteristic that changes is scale. In a cartoon, the accuracy of scale is missing. In its place comes a make-believe, unreal quality. Remember, though, that this unreal quality cannot be too unreal. You must walk a tightrope between the absurd and the believable. I want the viewer to smile at my illustrations, even to laugh a bit, but I do not want a comic-book illustration. Therefore, all the same rules apply, except that I exaggerate the scale.

This page
Pen and Ink
Two-ply Bristol Board
24 × 36 inches
Client: The New York Times
The layout for these drawings of Holland was done by taking a slide of a road map of Holland and then projecting the image on tracing paper and drawing it in pencil. Once the image was on tracing paper, we began to put in the cities, the windmills, roads, trees, and other details. These were all exaggerated upward in size, so that the viewer could recognize them and their locations. The trick is not to exaggerate so much that the drawing loses its credibility and becomes an actual cartoon.

Opposite
Pen and Ink
Two-ply Bristol Board
24 × 36 inches
Client: Brooklyn Museum
This illustration of Brooklyn was done with the same map technique used in the drawings of Holland. The only difference in this illustration is that the curve of the earth is shown with Manhattan on the horizon. This was the first time I tried this, and I liked it so much, I began to use it on all of my illustrations of this type.

138

Above
Pen and Ink
Double-thick Crescent Illustration
Board;   24 × 36 inches
Client: Albert Lorenz
This drawing layout was done by taking three overlapping photographs from the same point. Once the slides were processed, they were easily made into 8½ by 11 inch color Xeroxes. These three Xeroxes were then cut and rubber cemented together. This panoramic shot was then traced onto illustration board. We did this rather than using a wide-angle lens, since there is less distortion using this method. The drawing itself was done using three- and four-zero Rapidographs, in about one hundred hours.

Opposite, top
Pen and Ink
Two-ply Bristol Board
24 × 36 inches
Client: The River Café

Opposite, bottom
Pen and Ink
Two-ply Bristol Board
24 x 36 inches
Client: Southwest Publishing Co.
This view of a small town was done entirely freehand. The color in the original was applied with a brush and waterbase colored pencils.

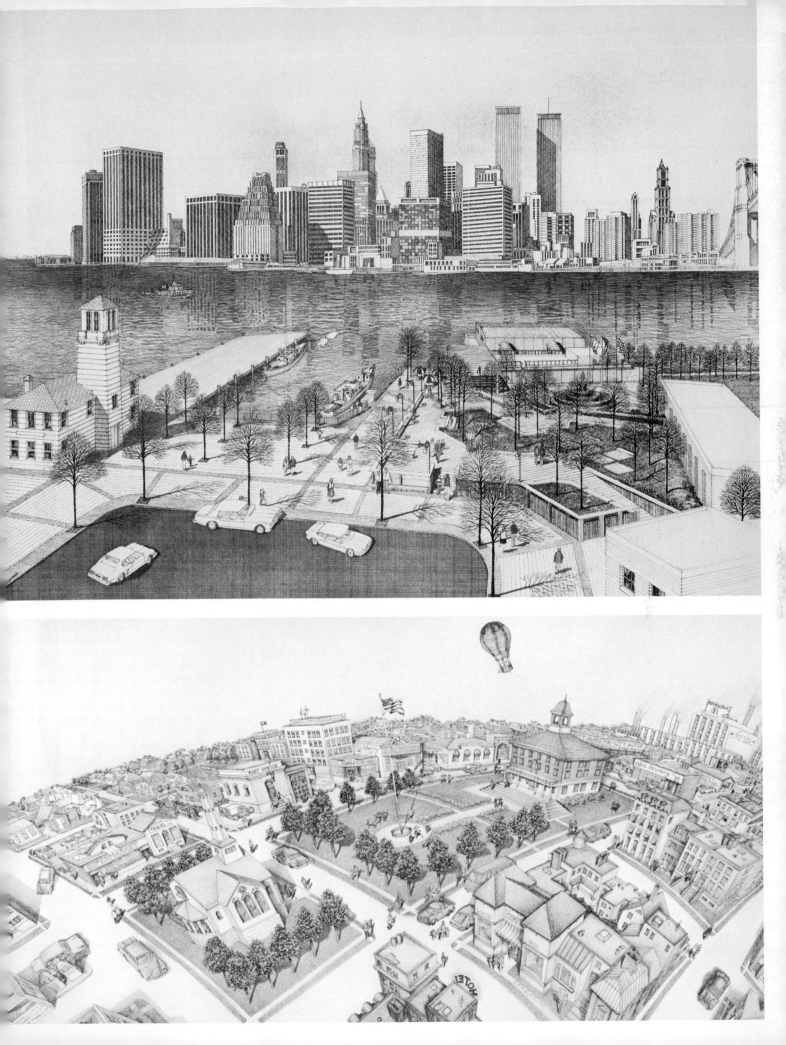

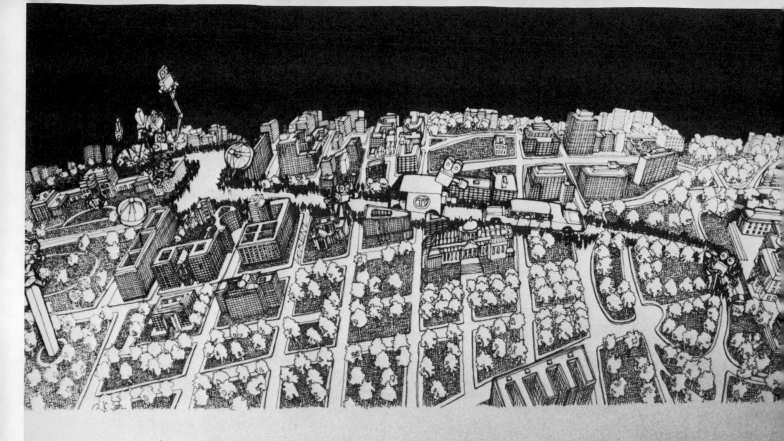

Pen and Ink
Two-ply Bristol Board
20 × 30 inches
Client: Lohman Advertising
Here is a pencil sketch and the finished version of the same drawing. As you can see, the pencil sketch is a very accurate one. Some illustrators like to present their clients with rather loose sketches. I like to be as accurate and as close to the finished product as possible. I find I have much less trouble with the client when I follow this route. Once the client gives me the go-ahead, I transfer my sketch to a piece of illustration board. In this case, the light table was used to transfer this drawing to a piece of two-ply Bristol board. It was then completed in pen and ink using a three-zero and four-zero Rapidograph. The amount of time spent on this drawing from start to finish, including client visits, was approximately sixty hours.

142

Pen and Ink
Two-ply Bristol Board
10 × 24 inches
Client: The Washington Star
This drawing was done in pen and ink in two days for *The Washington Star*. Whenever an illustrator has to work for a publication, be it newspaper, magazine, or other, there are usually very tight deadlines. With only two days to work, the style and the character of the linework must change. Compare this drawing to the Lohman drawing on the facing page to see what I mean.

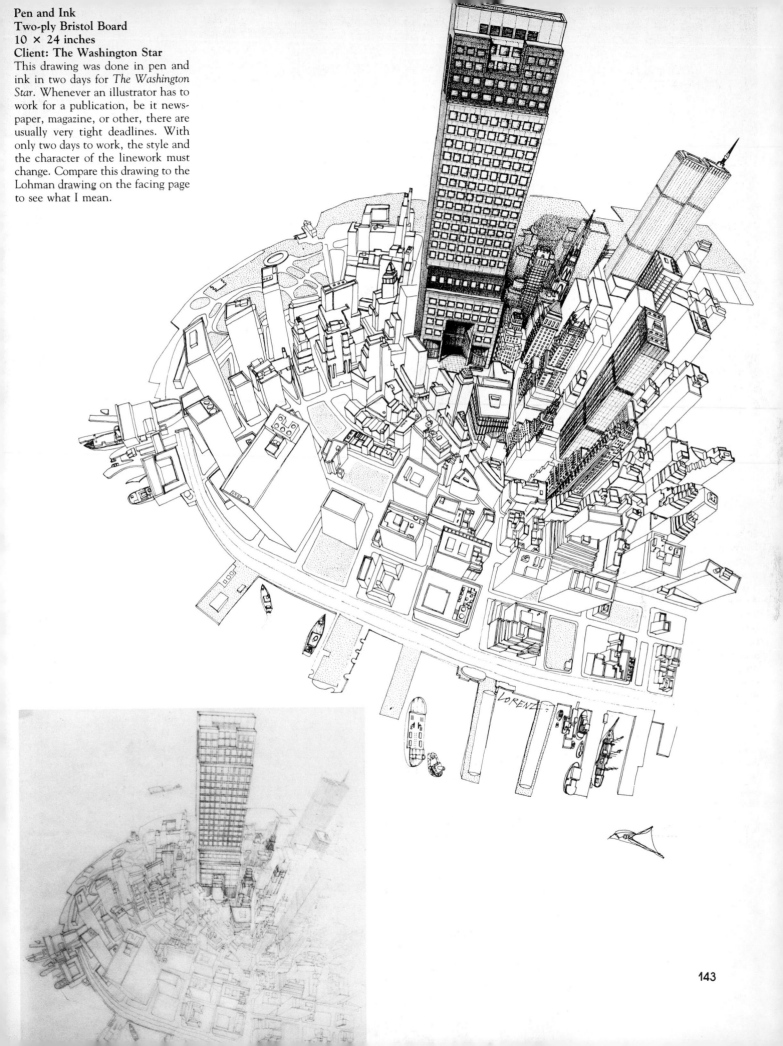

143

Preceding spread
Pen and Ink
Double-thick Crescent Illustration Board; 30 × 40 inches
Client: Albert Lorenz
This illustration took almost two hundred hours to complete. This is the kind of drawing I really enjoy doing. I think it has a subtle humor, but it is also a finely detailed drawing with quite a lot of architectural interest. To get and keep the viewer's attention, we drew the buildings of more importance with more detail and with a heavier pen. In addition, these are the only buildings treated with shade and shadow. The colors were then added by using a water-based colored pencil (Caran D'ache). The colors were lightly applied with the pencil and then a light wash of water was added over the pencil. The result is a very subtle wash of color. We used Pelikan waterproof ink so that the ink would not run when the wash was applied.

Above
Pen and Ink
Two-ply Bristol Board
8 × 20 inches
Client: Writer's Digest
This editorial was drawn for a magazine on writing, to illustrate an article about the problems of writing. Once again, this drawing was done entirely in line.

Left
Pen and Ink
Two-ply Bristol Board
8 × 10 inches
Client: Rizzo Advertising
This illustration was done with the stippling technique. It took about twenty hours to complete.

Opposite, top
Pen and Ink
Two-ply Bristol Board
20 × 30 inches
Client: Pratt Institute
Here is another editorial about city life, done in pen and ink. This drawing was done entirely in line, with no halftones used.

Opposite, bottom
Pen and Ink
Two-ply Bristol Board
20 × 30 inches
Client: Albert Lorenz
Another statement on city life, done in pen and ink, this drawing took approximately fifty hours to complete and was done entirely in line.

147

18. OVERVIEWS

Aerial perspectives, overviews, and bird's eyes are different names for the same thing: a drawing which places the viewer above the earth, as if in an airplane. The same rules apply in terms of layout as I explained in chapter 13. The one characteristic that all these drawings share is the use of a curving grid. Since these drawings are deliberately faked to produce the curvature of the earth, I must have a grid within which I can accurately spot buildings. This grid is created on an overlay piece of tracing paper. The dimensions are taken from the photograph, which gives me the approximate distance from one street to another. Once the grid is complete in both directions, it is a simple thing to spot the buildings. These drawings are extremely time-consuming. When you sit down to complete one of them, be ready to grow to your chair!

Below and opposite
Pen and Ink
Two-ply Bristol Board
24 × 36 inches
Client: Marriott Hotel
The Marriott Hotel is the only building which has been exaggerated. All of the other buildings are accurately drawn. The size of the building, and the fact that the color is more pronounced in the center of the illustration, help to pull the viewer's eye towards the Marriott building.

Next spread
Pen and Ink
Two-ply Bristol Board
24 × 36 inches
Client: Sail Magazine
The original size of this drawing is twenty inches by thirty inches. It was done to publicize and direct people around the America's Cup Races at Newport, R.I. The drawing was done freehand from a series of photographs.

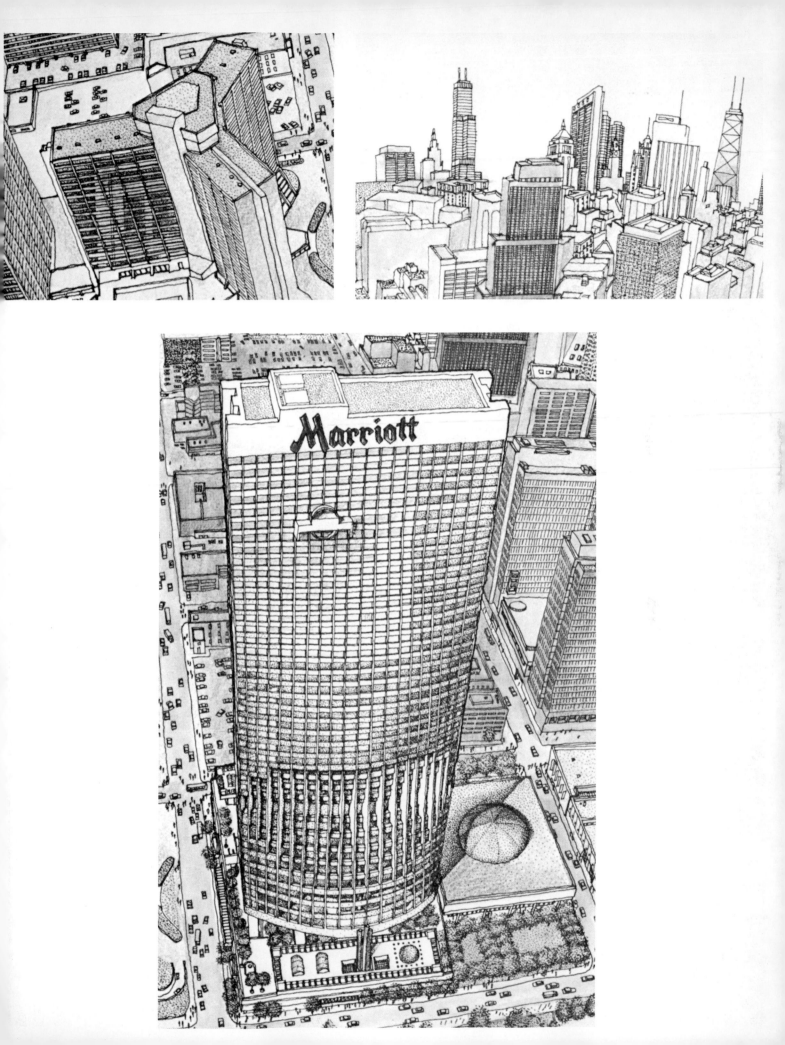

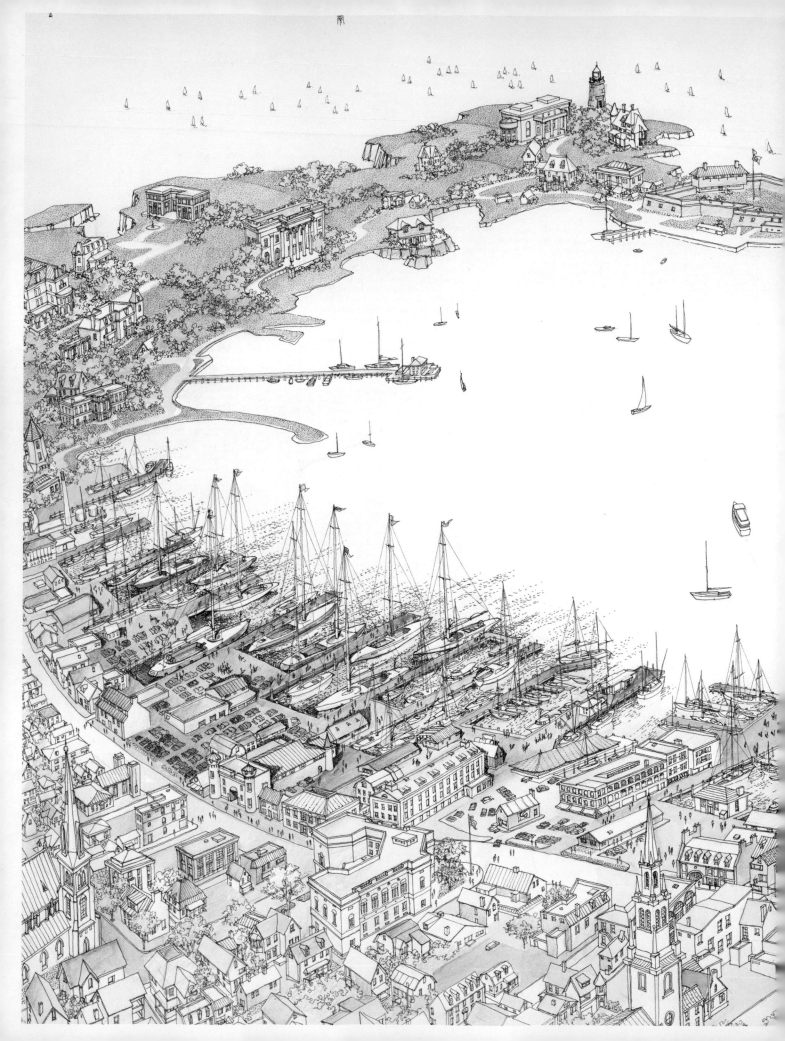

Left
Pen and Ink
Two-ply Bristol Board
30 x 40 inches
Client: The City of Columbus, Ohio
This aerial view of Columbus wa
done from a series of photograph
that were put together to form the
layout. The entire drawing was don
freehand; the color in the origina
was added using brush, waterbase
pencil, and airbrush.

Below
Pen and Ink
Two-ply Bristol Board
20 × 30 inches
Client: David Wachsman

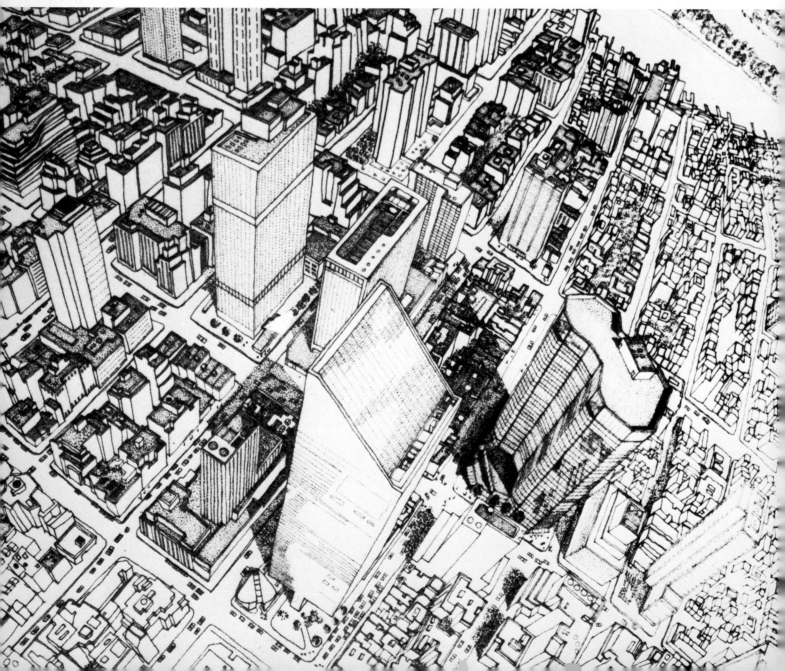

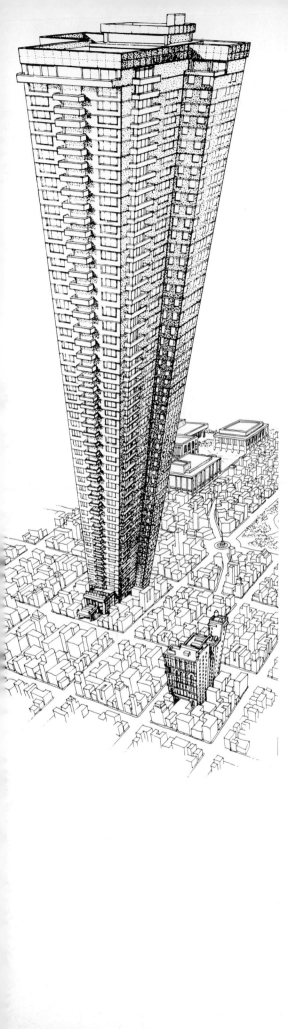

Left
Pen and Ink
Two-ply Bristol Board
10 × 15 inches
Client: Ogilvy & Mather

Below
Pen and Ink
Two-ply Bristol Board
15 × 20 inches
Client: Gips & Balkind
All of the drawings on this page and the facing page were done to show the relationship of a building or group of buildings to the surrounding area. The character of each illustration is different, depending upon the needs of the client.

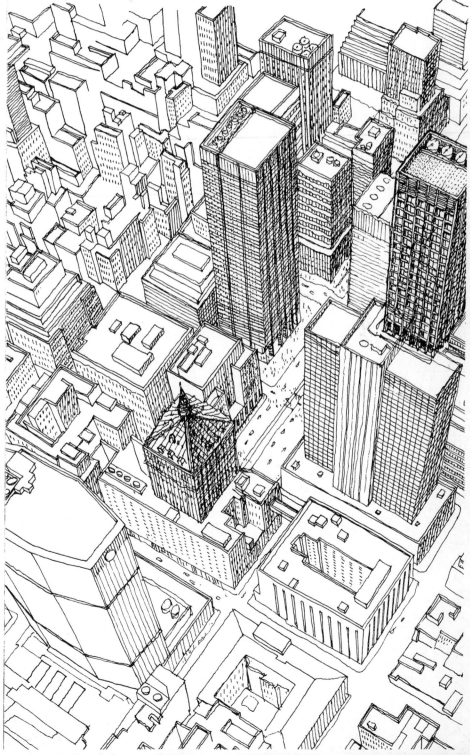

Pen and Ink
Two-ply Bristol Board
24 × 36 inches
Client: Ted Bates Advertising
These drawings were originally done in pen and ink, with a wash of watercolor in addition to an airbrush background. Once again, you can see how close the pencil sketch is to the final drawing.

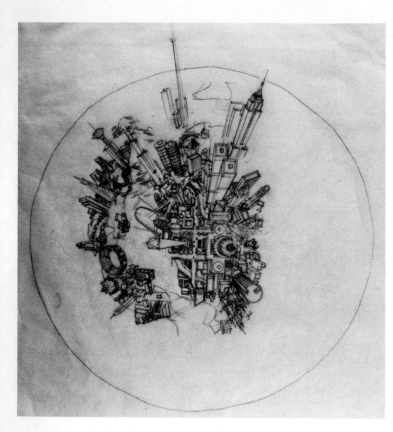

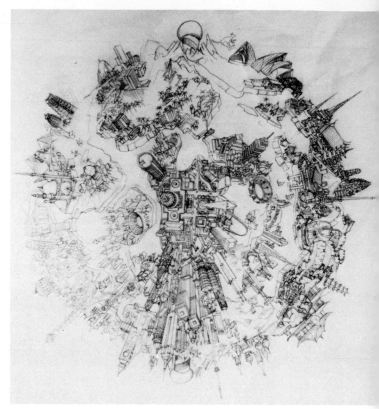

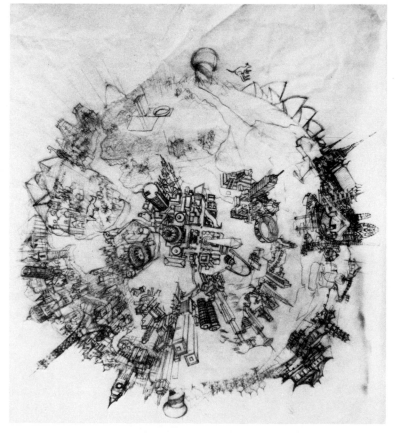

Pen and Ink
Two-ply Bristol Board
24 × 36 inches
Client: Wells Rich Greene
Advertising

Here we see just how this illustration was put together. The layout was done on tracing paper, in pencil. The details were then added, step by step. Once I was happy with the pencil sketches, and more importantly, the client was happy, the drawing was transferred to a piece of two-ply Bristol board. The ink work was done with a three-zero Rapidograph. The color (in the original) was added with water-base colored pencil and brush.

PAN AM HOLIDAY
WORLDBOOK
1984

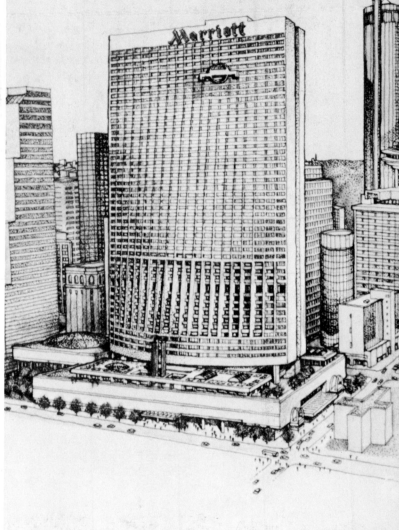

Pen and Ink
Two-ply Bristol Board
24 × 36 inches
Client: Marriott Hotel
This is another view of Atlanta. In this case, the client wanted a separate drawing of the Marriott Hotel that would be inserted into a brochure. The drawing was done freehand, with an overlay of watercolor pencil.

Pen and Ink
Albanene Tracing Paper
10 × 20 inches
Client: BBDO Advertising
I am always more at ease working within a grid, or some other kind of framework. As you can see by the pencil sketches, the drawing becomes rather elementary when all of the buildings work within this grid. Always try to simplify drawing and layout. Finish technique should be as simple as you can devise.

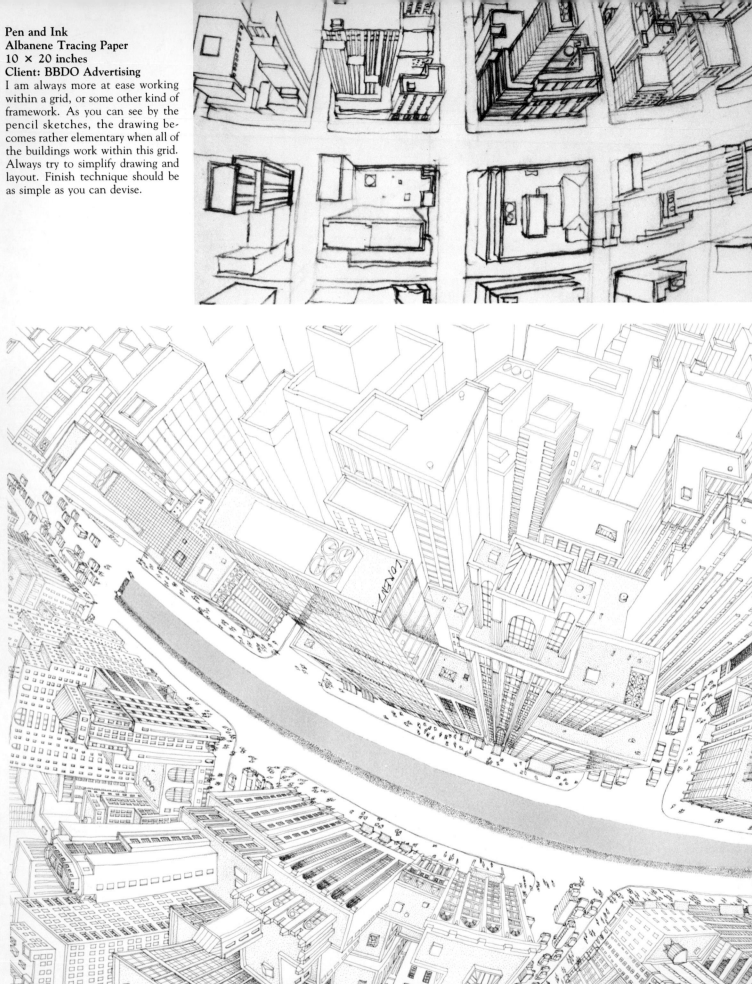

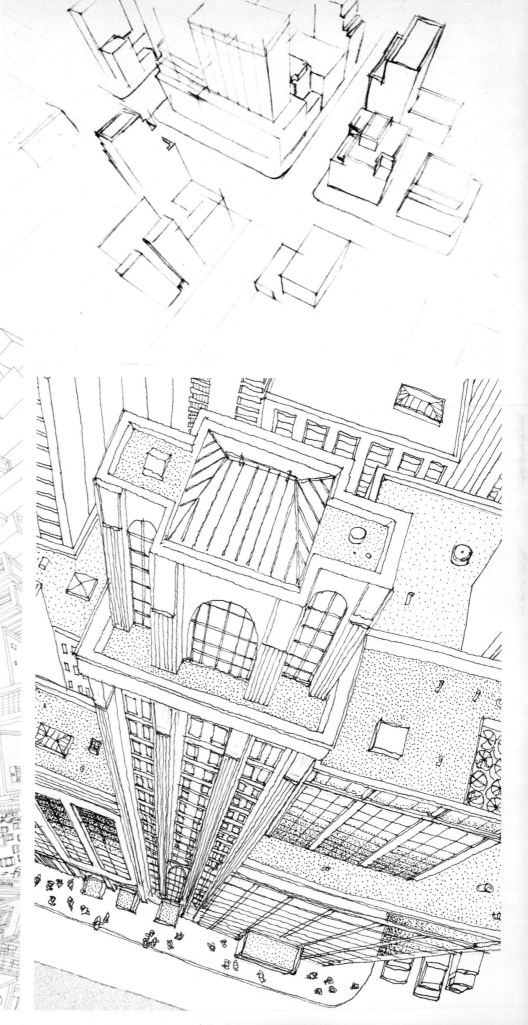

Next spread, left
Pen and Ink
Two-ply Bristol Board
24 × 36 inches
Client: Albert Lorenz

Next spread, right
Pen and Ink
Two-ply Bristol Board
24 × 36 inches
Client: Olympia & York
Note the difference in technique in these two aerial views of Manhattan done from slightly different directions. One drawing took twice as much time as the other. See if you can figure which took more time and why.

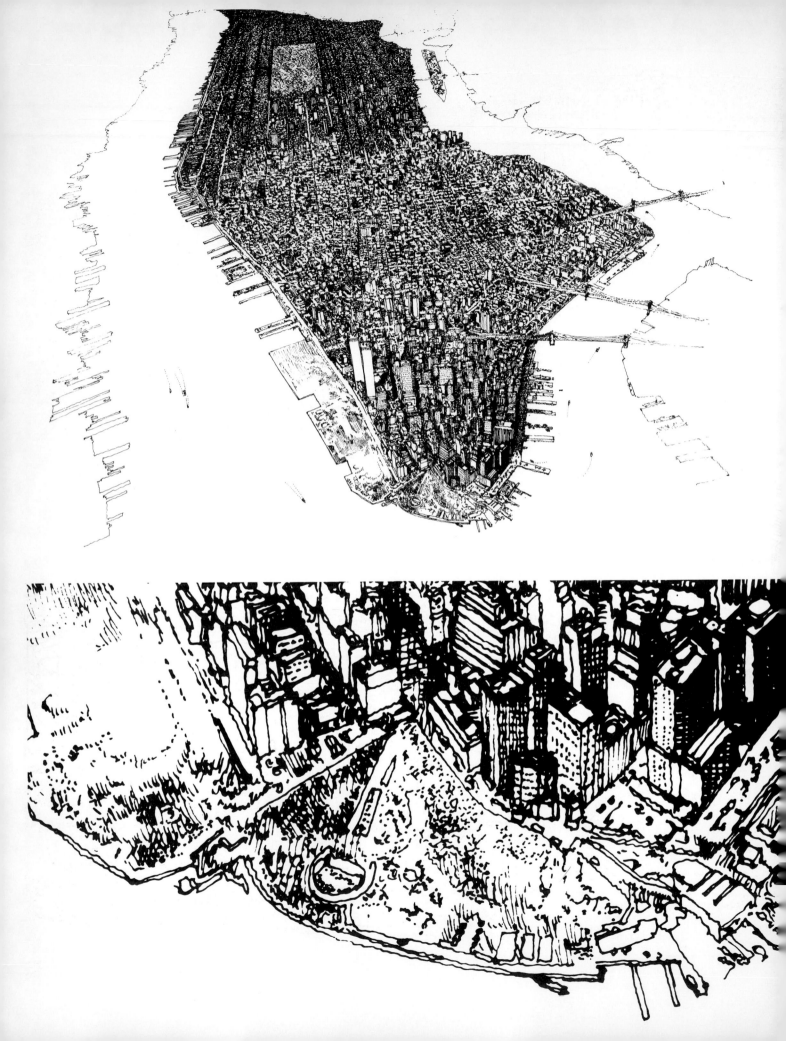

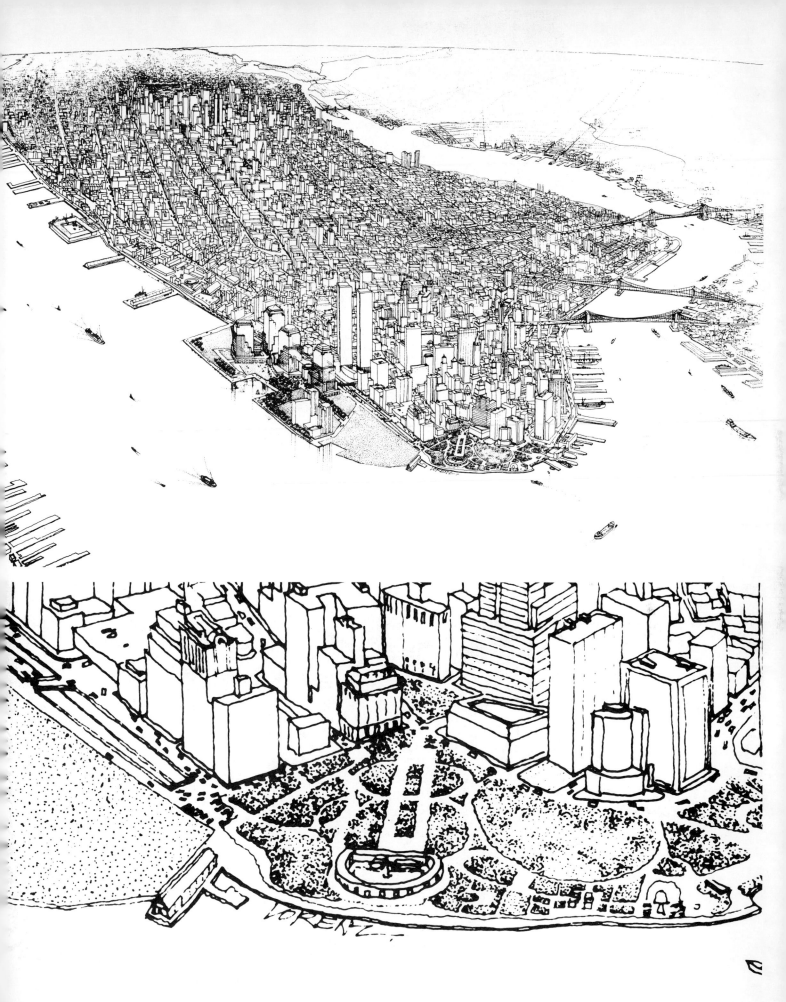

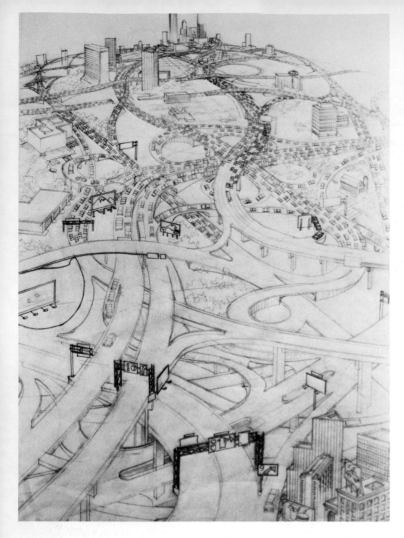

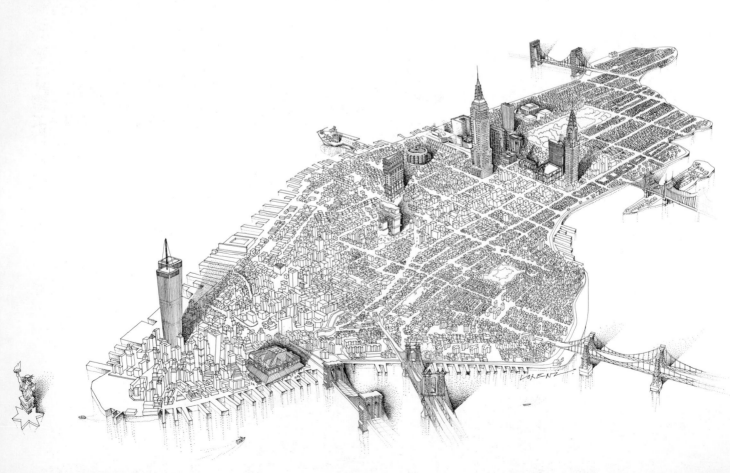

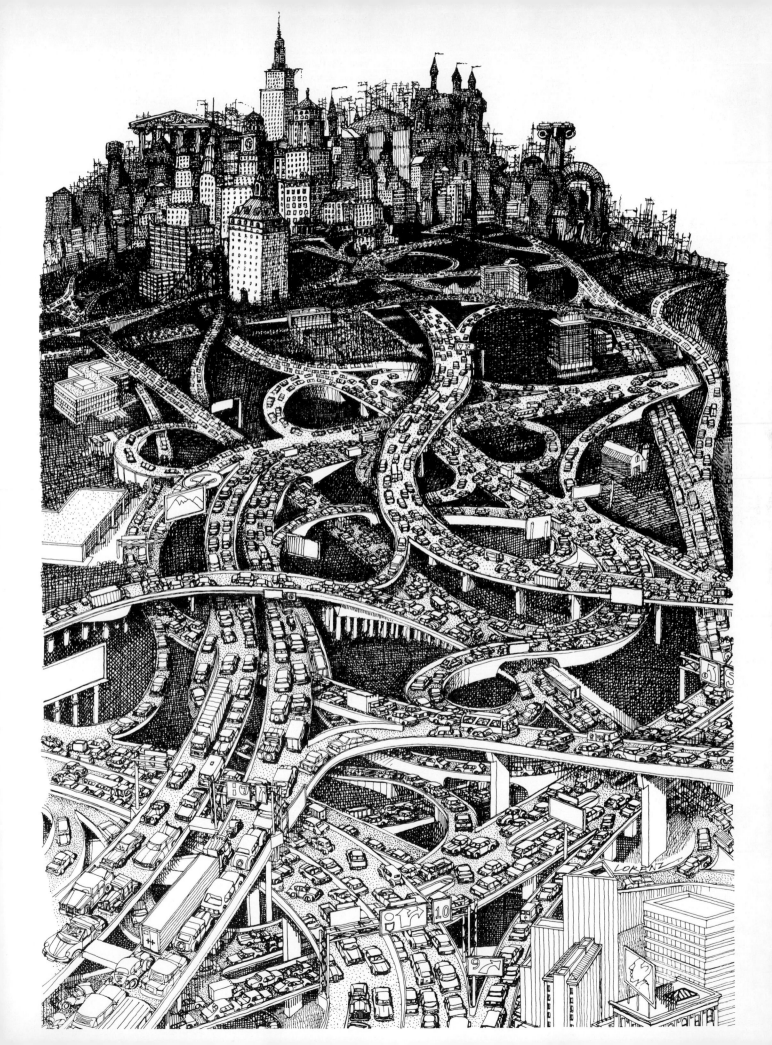

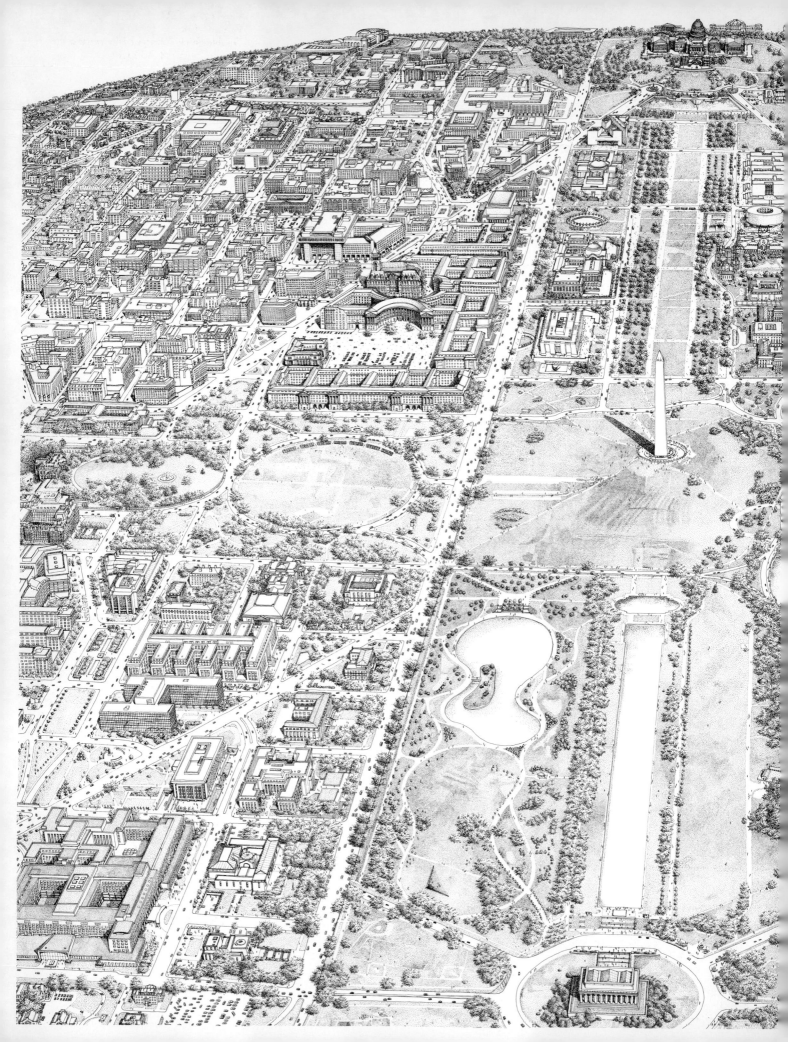

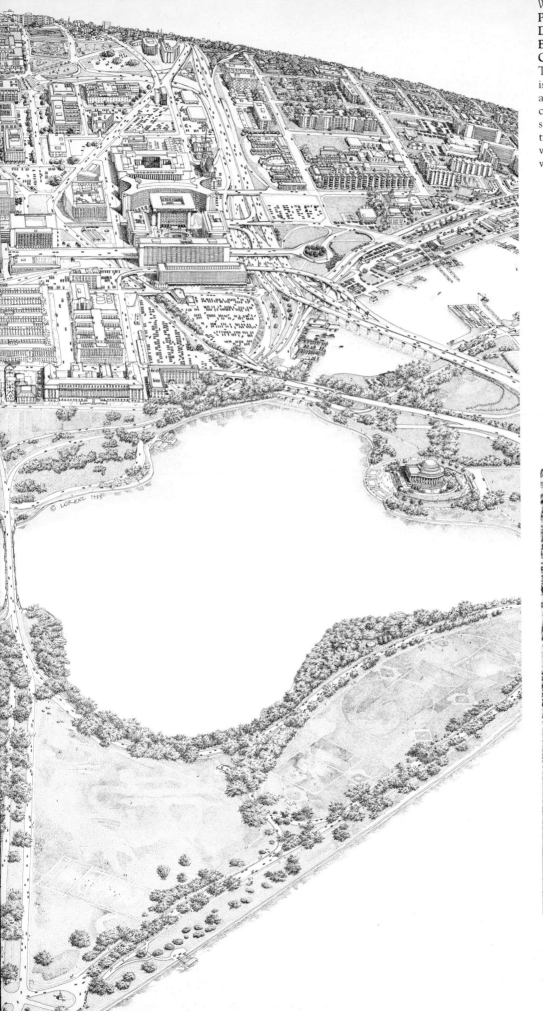

Washington, D.C.
Pen and Ink
Double-thick Crescent Illustration
Board; 30 × 40 inches
Client: Citivues
This overview of Washington, D.C.
is part of a series. This drawing took
approximately two hundred hours to
complete. It was done by projecting
slides of Washington onto the illustration board. Once the entire image
was drawn in 2H pencil, the inking
was completed.

Washington, D.C.—Details
Pen and Ink
Double-thick Crescent Illustration Board;   30 × 40 inches
Client: Citivues
These are the details of the Washington, D.C. overview. Note the line-work and the stippling. Remember how the two are combined to produce light, shade, and shadow.

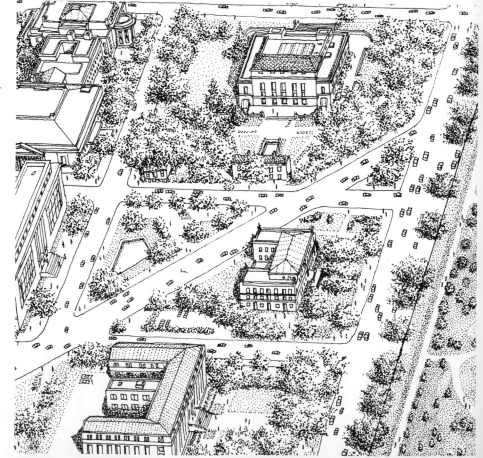

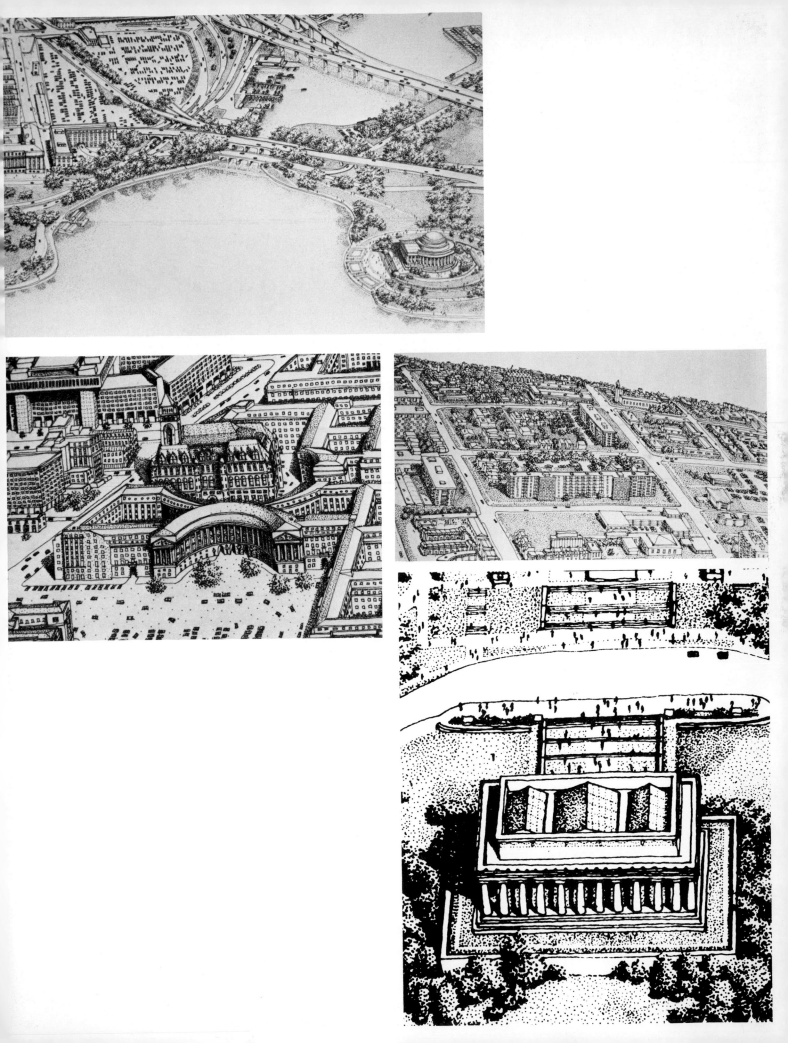

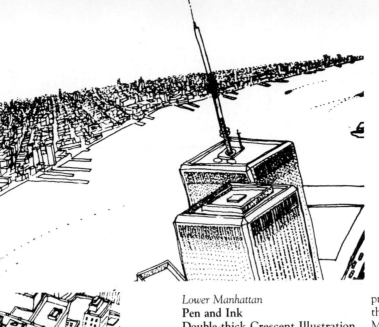

Lower Manhattan
Pen and Ink
Double-thick Crescent Illustration Board;   30 × 40 inches
Client: Citivues
Once again I used a camera to produce this layout. First, a series of aerial slides was taken. The slides were then overlapped so that when projected, they produced a mosaic that became the aerial view of lower Manhattan. After any inaccuracies in the pencil stage were corrected, the inking was begun. Approximately one hundred and eighty hours later the drawing was finished. The inking was done with three-, four-, and five-zero Rapidographs.

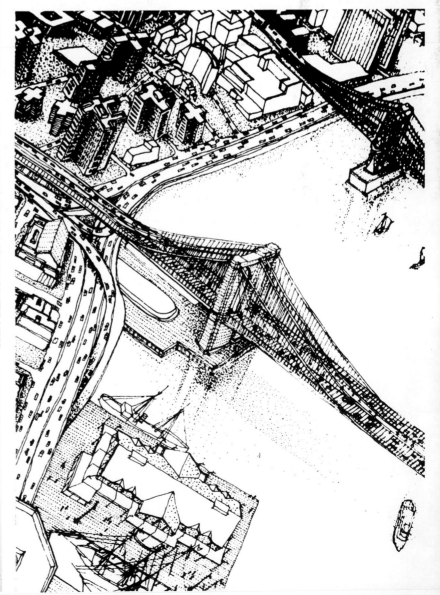

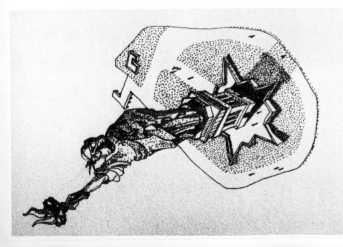

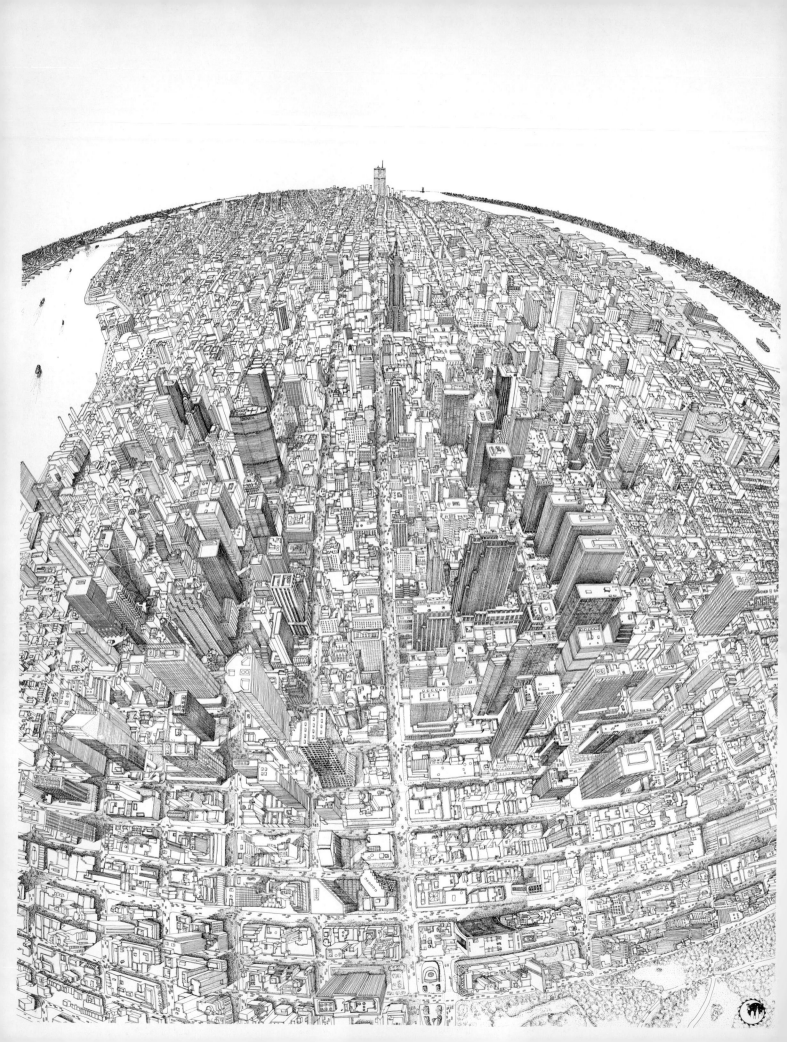

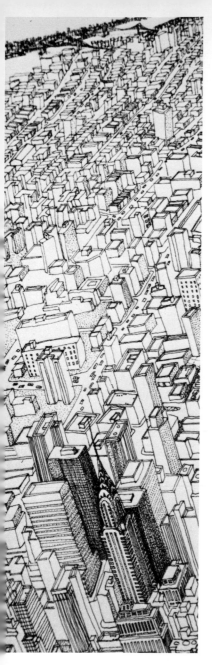

Midtown Manhattan
Pen and Ink
Double-thick Crescent Illustration Board;   30 × 40 inches
Client: Citivues
This drawing took over two hundred hours to complete. The linework was drawn freehand using three-, four-, and five-zero Rapidographs. The projection of slides was once again the method of layout. Note the method used in representing the reflections.

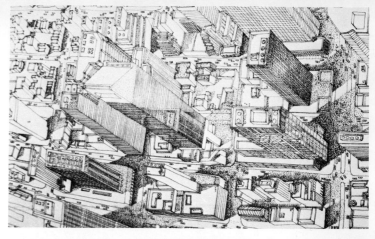

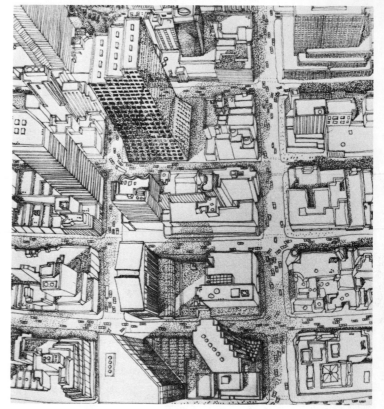

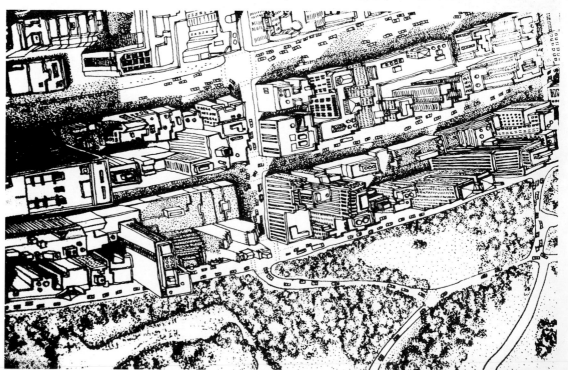

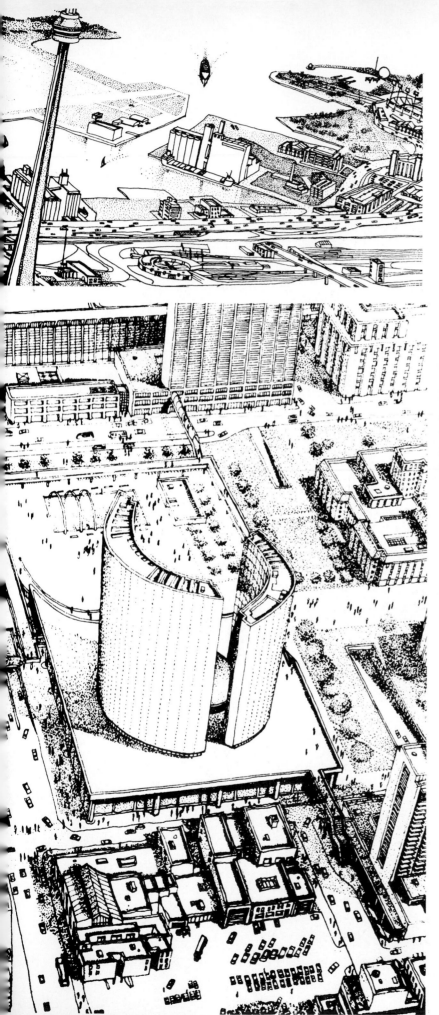

Toronto
Pen and Ink
Double-thick Crescent Illustration
Board;   30 × 40 inches
Client: Citivues
This drawing was done freehand in approximately one hundred and fifty hours. Once again three-, four-, and five-zero Rapidographs were used. In this drawing we tried to allow the viewer to look into buildings. In order to do this we drew the buildings as if there were no glass. This was done selectively on large buildings and spaces.

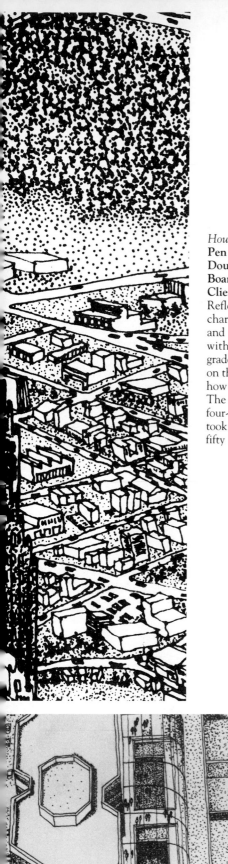

Houston
Pen and Ink
Double-thick Crescent Illustration
Board;   30 × 40 inches
Client: Citivues
Reflection is this drawing's strongest characteristic. The feeling of glass and multiple reflection was handled with stippling. The stippling was graded from dark to light depending on the tone of the reflection. Notice how carefully the dots were placed. The drawing was done using three-, four-, and five-zero Rapidographs. It took approximately one hundred and fifty hours to complete.

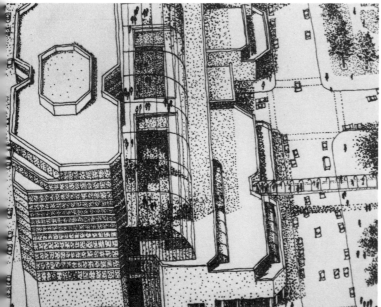

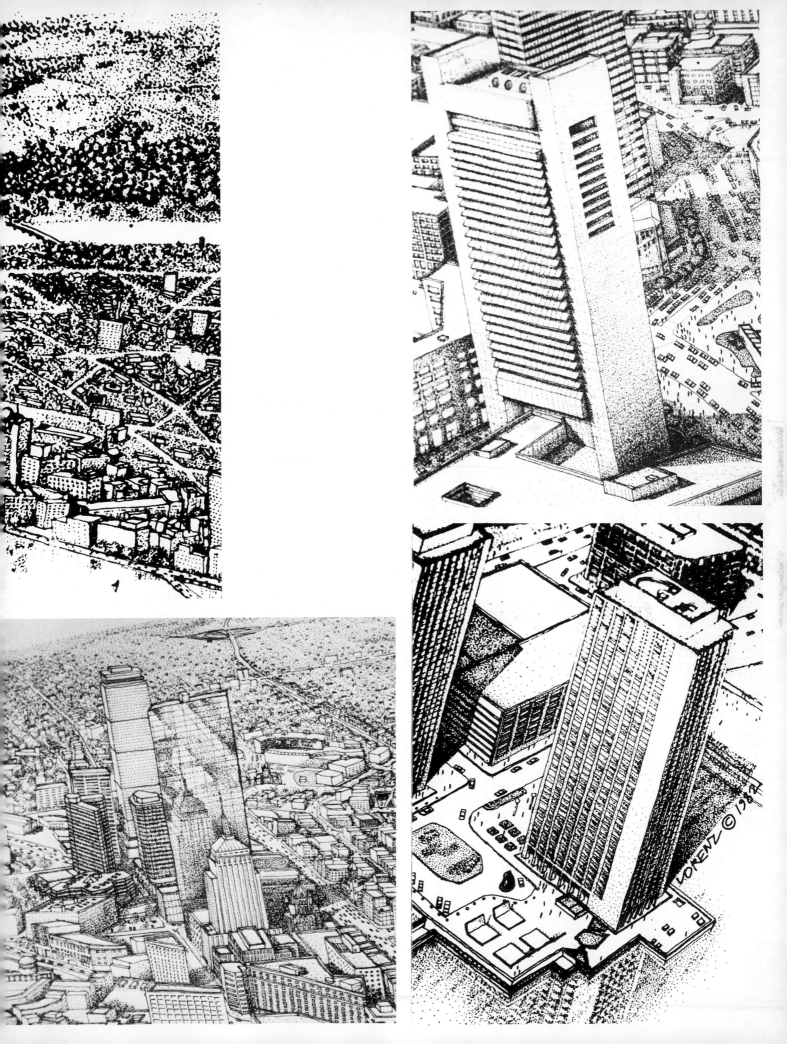

San Francisco
Pen and Ink
Double-thick Crescent Illustration Board;   30 × 40 inches
Client: Citivues
The outstanding characteristic of this illustration is contrast—the contrast of trees to architecture, and of water to land mass. The illustration was done using three-, four-, and five-zero Rapidographs. It took about two hundred hours to complete.

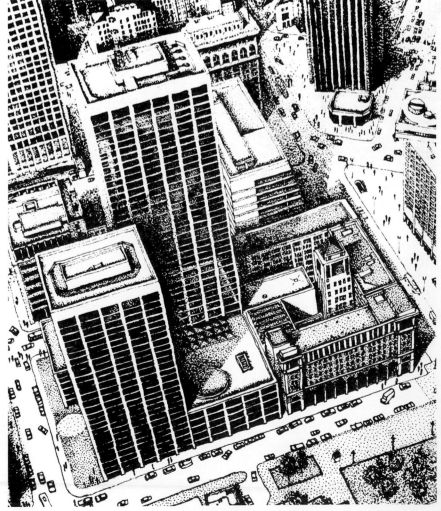

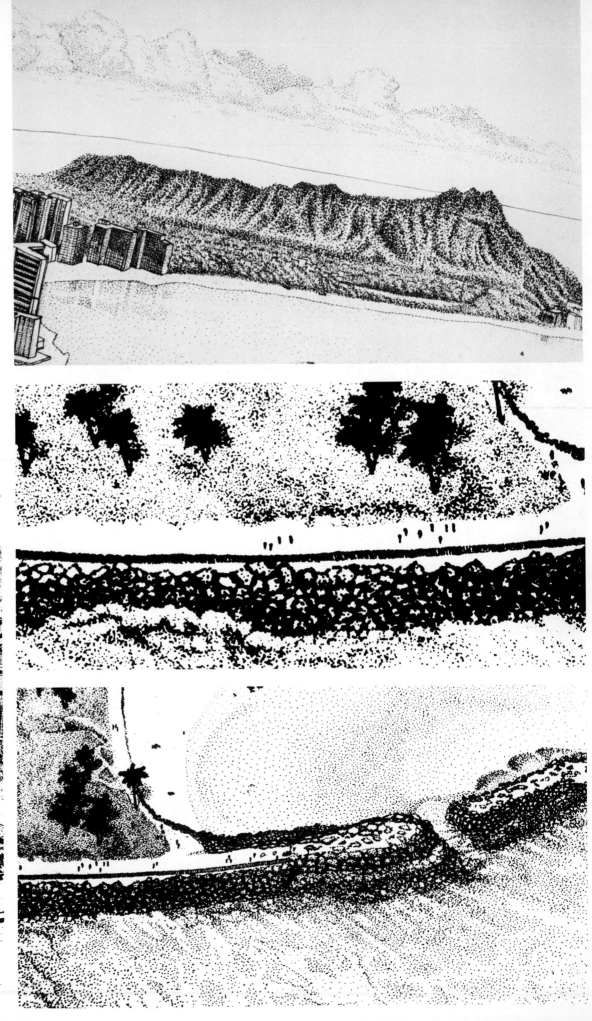

Waikiki
Pen and Ink
Double-thick Crescent Illustration
Board;   30 × 40 inches
Client: Citivues
This illustration is almost all water.
The difficulty was in delineating the
water, clouds, reefs, and sand. This
is the most subtle of all these aerial
drawings; it was also the most difficult. It was completed using a
three-, four-, and five-zero Rapidograph. It took two hundred hours to
finish.